METAMODERN DESIGN

AN OUTLOOK ON THE FUTURE OF DESIGN

JORDAN WAYNE LEE

For information contact;

Jordan Wayne Lee

jordan@jordanwlee.com

www.metamodern.ist   www.jordanwlee.com

Book and Cover design by Jordan Wayne Lee

www.jordanwlee.com

ISBN: 9798687112116

First Edition: September 2020

10 9 8 7 6 5 4 3 2 1

To the my Creator.
The universal Designer who gives us the beauty of life and humanity.

To my wife, Laura, you have shown me unconditional love and patience.
And how to become a voice for change, to have courage, to exist within
the uncomfortable places of myself and to never give up. I love you.

To my family and lifelong friends. For loving and supporting my
unconventional journey through life outside the 9-5 work cycle.

Contents

INTRODUCTION

T his book was written from a perspective over the past 13+ years of my experience working as a designer in both print and digital mediums across mobile, digital, web marketing, platform design, ux design, print design, brand identity design, responsive design, augmented reality design anvd environmental design for agencies, startups, global corporations, entrepreneurs, public figures, celebrities and entertainment companies.

Over the course of my career, I have worked across these various areas within design utilizing design thinking, processes and execution of work in collaboration with many others in the corporate global space, startups, small businesses and non-profits.

This writing serves as an exercise in thinking about design, the current landscape of design, and what might the future designer need to encompass for design to evolve and succeed amidst the changing global cultural landscape.

The idea of the term "metamodernism" serves as a framework to observe and describe a sensibility happening within culture. The first half of this book discusses views on design and culture and the last half explores how the designer might approach the future of design related to these observations. Within these two sections, I try to describe and articulate the ideas around "metamodernism" and how we came to be within that movement today.

It's been a long journey of success and failure within the work of design. This book is a collection of thoughts and observations collected over time through working on large and small design projects, leading teams, failing in startups, writing code, building apps, creating album art, designing brands and building platforms and campaigns for some of the biggest companies in the world.

This book doesn't provide specific answers to become a great designer through practice and technique, but provokes you to think about the observations laid out to create a new place to observe, think and find new ways to apply design for the future.

Defining Design

———

Design is not solely limited to our understanding in the visual, architectural or interactive sense. Design transcends the traditional ideas of the discipline and extends into a meaningful and purposeful approach to systems, thinking, digital, environmental, and development.

Design is about solving problems. The design process is about scaffolding your steps to discover the best solution for the challenge. I am a firm believer in a scaffolding approach where you discover, research, and then prototype to test and validate before creating a final design solution. The sum of those parts are all design, though many view the output as the definition of design.

Not just prototype an end product or service. I'm talking about prototyping the creative thinking to find the solution. Prototype your ideas and then explore all possibilities to make products or services from those ideas and align them to your early vision.

Design is problem solving

Design is problem solving. But with solving a problem, have we created others in the process? Why continue to design if the end result is a fleeting pursuit of constantly trying to fix and solve additional problems created from solving an initial problem? We cannot tackle all the world's problems. Or can we? And through what value system? Must we destroy the modern structures to build new ones? We must only solve problems that create a new sense of power through a postmodern lens?

All of these things should be measured differently.

Design is about envisioning a new future and building solutions to the challenges that keep us from the manifestation of that future. Looking at past problems, past best practices, past success, past failures and finding a way to navigate through compounding problems from flawed design over time to create better products or services.

But what if - designing better products, services and solutions for the future means building a better humanity in the present? What if better design isn't about building on top of the current societal systems of modernism and postmodernism, but applying both movements to our work in the sense of building a better structure of humanity.

Build a better self. Build a better existence. Build a better life. Build better design.

For example:
- •A poorly designed product can have the best intentions.
- •A struggling business can have beautiful design.
- •A great business with beautiful design can be successful.
- •A struggling business with poor design can fail.
- •A great business with beautiful design can fail.
- •A struggling business with poor design can succeed.

A modernist outlook would say that the success or failure of the design of the business is contingent on the strength of the system.

A postmodernist outlook would say that the success or failure of the design of the business is because of lack of support, lack of resources or the success is true, but not measured in dollars and profits.

Define A Designer

—

Defining a "Designer" can be a difficult task. The definition of "design" is a vague, misused and often misunderstood term in culture today. We often mistake "design" with aesthetic, beauty, art, look and feel, or something visual. However, design is an underlying premise, process and execution of a solution implemented in various ways to solve a challenge.

Design is not art. Design is not purely aesthetic. Design is not a singular attribute or tactic to a wider body of challenges.

Design exists as a solution within or beyond a system. Design seeks to find new and innovative ways to uncover all information (qualitative and quantitative) within a challenge and use that information to explore and define possible solutions to test and iterate upon through various processes until a positive solution can be discovered through valid confirmation. Design seeks to understand, and then use the understanding to step forward into discovering and implementing solutions.

Cultural majorities view design as a means to an end. A logo. A graphic. A website. A set of icons. A marketing campaign. All of these parts are integral to the process of design, however, design must look at the deeper underlying information to understand the challenge as a foundation and design through a process of discovering the right solution from that foundational challenge.

For example: Steve Jobs didn't inherently know that minimalist white clean design and inspiring messaging would help transform Apple in the 90's. This wasn't a tactic he used to get the masses to take notice of Apple as an innovative company. The end result we see in those products and marketing initiatives was a result of Steve Jobs understanding the depth of what he believed about the world, and what people wanted to believe about the world. The challenge was to inspire and create new innovative products that took humanity into a future that had not yet existed. The end result is a minimalist and beautiful product line combined with a marketing approach that reflected those deeply held beliefs.

I studied under Marty Neumeier, who was responsible for the execution and design class this we direction for Apple. He described Steve as being difficult at times. During the process they went through rounds and rounds of revisions until this different package leapt of the shelves because it was so different from all other packaging design during the time. The ability to embrace different and push boundaries was part of Apple's DNA.

Design is as much about reflection of the underlying beliefs as it is about coming up with new and interesting ways to create ideas and products. Designers must understand the DNA of the business, the challenge, the audience and the vision before creating an impactful solution.

In order to align and reflect the depths of a product, brand or service, we - as designers - must seek to go beyond the esoteric and aesthetically pleasing approaches and disciplines of our work, and truly seek to uncover the truth about a product, brand or service and use that discovery to inform the design approach for creating.

When people ask me what I do, there is usually a long answer that dives into the strategy and nuances and approach of my work with digital, brands or campaigns, but then there seems to be a default, shorter answer which usually sounds something like, "I'm a designer, I work in digital for a lot of different brands." And that usually ends that part of the conversation. Whereas, the alternative explanation better lends itself to you reading the rest of this work. Where I explain the depths and nuances of my work, or at the very least, my approach to the work.

I am not interested in educating you on how you should learn about design, or what tools to use, or even the foundational principles of design. Because I think those tools and information is easily accessible, and the landscape of design 20 years ago, the tools we used and the ideas we had look very different from today - and furthermore - the tools and ideas we will have about design 20 years from now will look much different than today.

However, I believe the idea of design and what a designer represents for society boils down to a few things. First, design is about systems and making things better for others. Designers take on the responsibility to discover the best possible solutions to fix problems within the world. Be it visual, experiential, environmental, economic, political, strategic, etc. Designers take on the hard responsibility of society and seek to make things better. Therefore, I do not believe my work here is designed (pun intended) for only those who chose the path of visual designer. I believe my thinking is meant for those in the boardroom, wall street, main street, entrepreneurs, social butterflys, artists, professors, and anyone who seeks to make the world a little better than when they started.

If you have ever solved a problem in life, you have partook in the act of design. If you have decided to commit your life to solving problems through systematic thinking, you are, in my definition, a designer - at the very least, did some kind of designing. Design is not limited to those who create visual work or visible products, but those who think deeply about the challenges that exist in the world and seek to solve them through resourceful means within their work and craft. The act of design transcends the definitions we have applied to them over the past century. Design is not limited to creative fields, but expands to systematic, engineering, business and economics as well. Design is difficult to define as a practice because it exists ubiquitously amongst our daily lives and therefore the act of design goes beyond the title of designer and finds its way into many variations of work. To be a designer is to seek to solve problems through the lens of making the world better for others.

Therefore, when I use the term "designer" or "design" in the context of my writing here, I am not thinking about a traditional form of design or designer, but the iteration of designers of tomorrow. I believe that there are foundational truths and principles of design that are beginning to emerge at a more prominent level of business, brands, economics, politics and influence within the world that has mostly been a way of thinking at a micro level of the practice of design. However, this nuanced level of approach, process and thinking when applied at larger scales is proving to be sustainable approaches to impact humanity at greater measurements.

Throughout my writing I share what I believe to be the evolution and iteration of a designer and how we can grapple with the changing landscape of design, focus this to a individual approach first and then apply this to the larger landscape of our work and our discipline. I am not going to focus on how to design, but more-so how we should approach our selfs by first addressing who we are as designers and how we can move forward into more global and larger impact by first focusing on the tenants of the self related to our work. We must choose to not only focus on the discipline and craft of our job as designing but inherently recognize the responsibility we have as designers and the growing role our work is having in our world.

Traditional definition of a designer

Traditionally, design derives itself within communication arts as an intention to create.

"It [Design] communicates to the viewer or user a visual and emotional message to change or guide through an emotional connection with a product or service enhancing their experience of the product or brand"

("Designer", 2020)

Design has changed over the years to account for the needs of mass production in society, whereas the intention of designing a product or service is directly related to cost of production. Within this area of production, design breaks down into specialized areas of the field of design.

As designer's progress within their careers, they begin to hone in on an area of specialization and a nuanced focused related to the work. Today we see design transcend many different areas of production such as Architecture, Costume design, Customer experience design, Experience design, Fashion design, Floral design, Furniture design, Game design, Graphic design, Industrial design, Interaction design, Interior design, Jewelry design, Landscape design, Learning design, Lighting design, Packaging design, Product design, Scenic design, Service design, Software design, Sound design, Strategic design, Textile design, Urban design, User experience design (which frequently includes mobile application design), User interface design, Visual design, Web design, Yacht design.

Design is a labor.

Design is an act.

Design is an intention.

Designer's exist within economics, business, politics, religion.

Design exists within every facet of our constructed society where one's job is to define or understand constraints, goals, research and make decisions. Design is not limited to the physical manifestation of a product or service, but the intentional act of creating better systems in the world.

Collectively, design can be found within the fields outside of the "creative" realm and manifest itself in the forms of economics, business, politics, religion, manufacturing, agriculture and technology. Design is the ability to understand the constraints, goals and information and create new or improved systems within these parameters.

There is a myth that design is "left to the designer's". The "creative" types that no one really understands and their job is to consistently make magic happen through design. However, this is not the case, and I believe we have operated in a culture where this intentional act of solving problems has been misconstrued with some form of "creative magic" only to be sparked and fostered within the expectations design and "creative" culture infused with ping-pong tables, beer on tap and free lunch.

But this fostering of culture is not the inherent driver of success (or failure) of design. Instead, we should seek to understand what design is at the micro-level of our thinking, approach and process; and then let these ideals permeate themselves throughout a culture or body of people who do not work specifically within the discipline of design, but to shift the thinking of those who do not believe they are "creative".

After working for close to two decades in corporate environments, startups, agencies and running my own business, I have come to the understanding that everyone is capable of design. But, the act and discipline of design requires a deep understanding of the tools and experience to execute. It also requires the ability to work with people collaboratively. However, within the initial part of understanding goals, constraints, and research, design tends to fall flat into the ever growing abyss of failure. Whereas, the actual intentions of defining goals, constraints and gathering information requires some design within itself - and this is where my belief derives. Design is not hinged within the culture, environment or amount of free lunches, but to look closely at the process and how we define initial foundations of our work - the information and discovery - that informs the success or failure of the actual act of designing.

We must seek to think about our process of defining constraints, setting goals and understanding clear objectives as an act of design within itself. These parts of our work go unseen in the end product or service, but they greatly inform the environment of our mental space in which we seek to define an end product. These initial parts are not limited to the responsibility of the designer, but through a collective of disciplines and experts in multiple fields to help define and clarify goals, objectives, strategies and research information. It is our job to ask questions, gain understandings and hold this part of the process responsible for never leaving any stone unturned. We must seek to examine all aspects, ask questions, and pull the information needed to see the entire landscape of a company or project before diving into our nuanced view of executing design.

Design is to create.

For decades, design has been placed as another expense on the assembly-line-conveyor-belt-of-mass-corporate-production. An added cost to make something look good and get it out the door. The success or failure then rides solely on the designer to deliver (or not deliver) on a product or service and then they reap all the glory or take the brunt of the blame.

However, as the Industrial Revolution has propelled us into the future of the early 21st century, design has articulated it's value from an economical, ergonomical and cost effective solution. Into the 21st century, we have found that the value of design has somehow transformed us out of the dark ages and into a society of productivity and consumerism.

Whether it be the rise or fall of the influence of design.

We forged new frontiers in technology and innovation with the implementation of design into software, hardware and technological products. We became inspired by these designs that unlocked doors of communication and endless possibilities of a transition into global commerce and communication systems for humans to share ideas. New forms of doing business and pushing new boundaries of innovation and creativity emerged.

We saw the era of Web 2.0 emerge from the bust of the dot-com boom in the late 90's. And the next step was to innovate and find new ways for us to utilize technology - all attractive, mysterious and elusive to mainstream society. This thing (tech, the internet, the web) was a designed system and we became like moths to the light.

Emerging from this opportunity came Google, Facebook, Apple, Amazon, Netlifx, Microsoft (FAANGM) and other industries adopted this technology. We gather our insights, news, communication, business and connectivity from a designed system built from the processes of design dating back to the Industrial Revolution.

With this, we also garnered amplified problems along the way.
- Social divide
- Cyber bullying
- Trolling
- Identity theft

- Cyber crimes
- Drug trafficking
- Sex trafficking
- Depression
- Sexualization glorification via social media
- Sex crimes
- Suicide from online activity
- Self-image issues
- Hate and racism
- Identity politics

The future of design will not look like the current landscape of design. And our current landscape has been informed by the past cycles of revolutions. Our current processes and understandings were born out of the notion to explore the details with design itself. The fundamental truths of design and the essence in which design derives it's value.

However, our future will not look like today - as the same way our present understanding and perspective of design does not look like our past. The thread is that design has and will continue to shape culture. Finding the meaning and purpose to shape our future is where I seek to uncover meaning and truths about what the landscape of design might look like in the coming years.

The term "designer" in this text is not limited to those who work within a discipline of design from the traditional definition. My intention is that "designer" means the "designer" which exists within all of us, and that must be articulated and defined throughout this work.

Design is systematic thinking to solve challenges and create new opportunities which improve the lives of others.

Design is the ability to connect the solutions and the audience in which a system serves and align these with the intentions of the business or brand.

Design seeks to execute within constraints to mitigate risk, minimize poor user experience and delight the audience throughout the interactions.

Therefore, with each of these defined, design is not limited to those who partake in the act of designing an end product or service from a traditional definition. But the act of design derives itself from the preparation and thinking about solving problems from many different disciplines. I believe that design is found within all parts of work and labor in which an individual or organization seeks to improve a system, or intentionally create something innovative. The complex parts within the system can only derive themselves with understanding the complex information that connects each piece of the system. Therefore, everyone involved in these endeavors takes on a role of design in one sense or another. It becomes the designer's job today and into the future to facilitate the act and intention of design within the collective disciplines of many to uncover the constraints, understand the goals, define the objectives and determine a strategy.

There may be work that has been done from various disciplines to articulate and define these things. Business leaders break down the goals and objectives, financial leaders seek to crunch numbers where things make sense to pursue, etc. However, the ability to look at these parts and serve as a liaison to the audience, define the needs of the audience, and translate the goals and intentions of the business or brand is where the designer takes on new responsibilities to make sure that the perspective and lens in which a business or brand is viewing these aspects are from a place of empathy and understanding to meet the needs of others.

The term "designer" is loosely defined and understood. With no barrier to entry for tools to practice design and no need for education to learn the foundations of design, the ease of picking up the digital design hammer and building your own body of work is easier today than going to your local hardware store and buying a screwdriver. The misconception and responsibility we have to design is greater than ever. The lack of intention and ethics around how and what we design is more important to understand now than any time in history. We bear a great burden.

On top of this we have created some new and rather interesting design job titles such as:

Producer of Experiences, Designer of Diversity, Interdisciplinary Technican of Design, Designer of Symptoms, Composer for Symbolism, Leader of Design Communications, Full-Stack Design of User State Regularity, Design Conductor, Designer and Entry-Level Generalist, In-House Designer of Composition, Staff Designer, Deputy and Intermedia Designer, Dream Alchemist, Creativity Analyst, Design Ambassador, Creator of Happiness

These pseudo-intellectual jargonist titles are a few examples within the design industry. They are whimsical and obscure to continue adding vague meaning behind the actual intention we really miss about what design is and how we can apply the meaning and purpose of design to our work.

The definitions of these titles around design are evolving and changing. Each designer is different whereas the standards and expectations of titles are not widely understood.

A dentist holds a set standard of operation.
A doctor maintains a standard.

A pilot flying a plane must be able to take-off, fly correctly and safely land. There are expectations within these fields that help others, progress society and lead people to destinations.

Design is no different. However, there is little expectation of the role of a designer within an organization outside of the work exemplified on a portfolio. It is the approach, process and strategic thinking of a designer in which does not get defined. The variance is great between designers (related to time in the field, experience and past projects) and it becomes an abstract topic to discuss the value design brings - whereas the difference between a junior designer and an Creative Director should be massively different, but there is no set bar to differentiate them within society.

Design, as it grows more into multidisciplinary work for the designer across print, identity and digital mediums comes closer to art and the designer referred more as an artist due to the lack of clarification on the designer's role as practitioner, workman, and thinker in society - socially, culturally, politically, and economically.

A designer, in whatever discipline, (but especially in digital) engages in creating solid/concrete design based on fundamentals established over decades and centuries of the practice - only to knowingly accept that the design will change, shift and morph itself whether by the bastardization of development or from the results of AB testing and the learning from data/research - or an update to the design after years of additional work by the same designer or a team of other designers. A concrete approach with known fundamentals to a fluid process and end result created an oscillation within itself from designing work with passion, sincerity, and empathy to understanding the underlying sentiment of irony that this work will inevitably change or completely disappear, no matter what.

To me, this experience, strategy, process and set of emotions defines metamodernism towards design. The oscillation between two poles (modernism and post-modernism) and having enough self-awareness to understand and accept the differences, regardless of personal preference.

There is a constant struggle between the designer and society where the view of the designer is seen as a workman, a hammer swinger, the last stop on the creative subway. Whereas, designers see themselves as providing deeper meaning, powerful thinking and strategy behind every choice of a design. The emotive dance between the perception of the designer and the reality of the work has created a struggling paradigm between the designer as a worker, and the designer as a thinker.

The value of design has always been exemplified through history as the immediate visual communication to modern culture. Designers have been at the forefront of culture, thinking, and progress. And this progression has led society to be inundated with technology, tools and social platforms for every person on earth with access to the internet to be part of this cultural immediacy. The over saturation of design begins to drown out the value of the designer. But, I believe, for the designer to survive, we acknowledge not only the oscillation of our work between being the Workman versus being the Thinker, but also the oscillation of the perceived value within society.

Humanize.

Design has always been a slight step outside of the lens of society, peering in ever-so cautiously and making commentary in visual, systematic, economic, human-driven dialogue. The irony of music, art and the cynical undertones as a commentary about the rise or fall of culture and society has plagued the design community for decades. Even so, being a designer has often been thought as being a lesser version of an artist, whereas they are equal, with differing points of strategy, thought and approach; yet culturally, design has not been as emotive, progressive or influential as an artist in the eyes of society.

Design is everywhere and it exists in everything we do. Our governments, our economy, our cities, and our daily aspects of life are all things that have been designed in some way or another - visual design is a merely a facet of the same kind of strategic thinking meant to be effective and solve problems. Through visual mediums, this is done through concise and clear means of communicating an idea to our audience. This type of thinking can be translated across all types of problem solving areas and is why designers are having a seat at the bigger tables of society and culture - because we solve problems and there is a return on that investment of thought patterns. You can apply the thinking patterns of a visual designer to most other problem solving areas and you will find that the designer will look for the patterns and find ways to circumvent the standard approaches to explore new and effective ways of thinking and solving problems.

The emerging of the singular designer/artist in society today creates an interesting oscillation of turbulent emotions in work. Uncomfortable. Whereas, design is meant to solve problems and art is meant to create problems; the merging of design and art as a single existence to work is a metamodern approach of how we function within both roles.

Breaking free from being the outsider of culture; a shift is happening within design. Design is becoming more prominent and leading progressive strategy and innovative approaches for business and culture.

Acknowledging the disconnect over the past few decades within a postmodern world and applying true sincerity from disconnecting the cynical emotions within our approach, to placing empathy and compassion at the center of work that is meant to evoke, disturb and question everything around us for the sake of moving forward in both irony and sincerity.

Versus being a designer or artist looking in from the outskirts of society and creating this ironic commentary on culture, it is the designer's job to marry the approach of design and art to function from being at the postmodern outskirts of culture, to shifting as the central point of focus for how we move forward.

Humanize everything.

The fear of the postmodern design approach is gone. We do not exist in that space anymore. And for the sake of our own survival, we cannot exist in that space. We must forge ahead as leaders of culture. We must take the dissonance of what used to be, and reflect on where we are going and force ourselves into the uncomfortable space between art and design.

Humanize ourselves. Humanize the work.

Culture depends on it.

As Jasper Morrison articulates his idea of design in The Unimportance of Form 1991, he states:

"The designer is often seen as a giver of form to an industry whose technological expertise will allow production. Like most things it's not that simple and in this case there can be no text book approach to a particular problem, solutions are always arrived at in unexpected ways. Occasionally a form will arrive, either through hard analysis or, more satisfyingly, intuition and chance. Restricting the probability of finding appropriate form to these two unreliable sources is a mistake. It's a fact that the physical appearance of an object is to most people most of that object's presence, but perhaps too much importance is attached to it. If we thought form less important we might develop a sensibility for other qualities in an object. Designing in a way that allows other aspects of an object's make-up to propose its form may be a step in the right direction. If we think of design as an equation for getting more from objects then it's clear that an approach which relies on gratuitous

novelty of form is not enough. Avoiding the issue of form altogether may provide a truer solution. The formal appearance of an object need not be the result of hours of careful analysis of the problem or pages of drawings. It could be the visual consequence of an idea, a process, a material, a function or a feeling. Then again it could arrive in the shape of a borrowed form or a stolen object. There can be no moral objection to this if the result contains something that wasn't there before. In fact the hi-jacking of everyday objects serves a dual-purpose of providing a new object in an economical manner and making the point that there is great beauty in the obvious or everyday. So describing the designer as a form-giver is inaccurate, he may be this but not only this and the less he concerns himself with creating form the better for all of us."

The pendulum of aesthetic.

Design movements seem to swing like a pendulum. Back and forth. Minimalism, modern, sleek design, skeuomorphism, flat design, etc. is poised throughout our culture from the hands of designers across the globe. This ripple effect takes place every few years and we see a shift of a certain aesthetic breaking away from a past trend across various types of mediums, marketing campaigns, product designs, etc.

At any point in time, a designer could walk down the street and more than likely decipher the type of product, message, or campaign something was designed for purely based on the architecture and composition of the aesthetic. The color, font style, texture, photography treatment and con-struct of a design can quickly render itself to being a groupthink aesthetic within various industries at certain points in time.

Examples:
- Trajan Pro as the movie font
- Bright gradients for anything related to the music industry
- Lifestyle campaigns for automotive commercials
- Minimalism for technology products
- Web design as flat design
- Skeuomorphic digital design for SaSS
- Handwritten fonts and natural colors for boutique consumer products

This pendulum seems to swing back and forth faster and faster. From the minimalist Swiss influenced modern approach of the Bauhaus era of design, to the reckless and abandon-all-rules of the ever chaotic approach of the 90's. Somewhere between the two, we find the aesthetic of various designers who have garnered their own sense of style by focusing strictly on either side of the pendulum, or creatively balancing the two within their personal work.

The 90's saw a group of designers who threw out all conventional design thinking influenced by the Swiss or Bauhaus modern movement and set out to disrupt every piece of visual they could get their hands on. Magazines, posters and prints during this time looked chaotic and completely destroyed. The visual language was oscillating and finding some sort of balance from all of the clean and minimalist designs that saturated the markets. Helvetica was an outcast during this time. Primary colors were disregarded. It was a playground of grunge and texture and disturbance. It was reminiscent of the culture - it resonated with the music, fashion, art and literature of the time.

And this pattern continued until the late nineties when Steve Jobs launched the visuals for Apple and the introduction to the iPod. The clean and minimal approach was back, with a notion of evangelical tones and a zen-like approach to the visual brand. The pendulum was swinging back and soon every tech company was copying the aesthetic because it was dominating the market.

And on and on, this happens constantly throughout culture.

(See 90's design examples: Storm Thurgeson, Ray-Gun, David Carson, Sub Pop Records album art, Quentin Tarantino film posters, Stefan Sagmeister, Nine Inch Nails, Keiji Itoh, Paula Scher)

Further Reading: "The Decade of Dirty Design" https://www.aiga.org/ the-decade-of-dirty-design

Commerce, business, commercialism and sales tend to drive the swinging aesthetic pendulum back and forth. Designers either follow an aesthetic that is working at the time to provide; or they have bought enough time to explore, experiment and begin swinging the aesthetic pendulum back the other way; if the sales follow, then so does the industry aesthetic.

Instead of bouncing back and forth, ever so often between these two dichotomies of design; clean vs. chaos. I believe visually, the true effectiveness of design lies somewhere in the moment where we can oscillate both at the same time. Presenting a clean product or brand in a very rough and distorted way. Or... a very dismal and chaotic product or work designed in a clean, minimal and modern way. To me, what I am trying to describe here, is that designer's need to pay attention to the messaging and tone of the brand and product itself and use the visual approach to create the tension within the product, campaign or message. This approach creates an oscillation of a metamodernist sensibility to the work, and in turn, is more effective than the constant swinging of the aesthetic pendulum. It's a difficult approach to execute, but if done correctly, I believe has the biggest impact to resonate with our future audience.

Through the lens of design.

The responsibility of being a designer is greater than ever. The impact design has on other's lives through a lens of metamodernism becomes the measuring stick. Metamodernism describes cultural values that we've been trying to make sense of for decades. It becomes a way defining modern humanity through observation of sensibilities and movements.

We must be willing to go deeper within ourselves to ask the tough questions. Outside of the lens of modernism or postmodernism. But to ask "both/and" at the same time.

The practice of design has changed and evolved over time. We cannot assume that the varying definitions and practices of design today will be the definitions and practice of design in the future.

As much as the digital revolution has changed the landscape of design and designers, the future will also introduce new platforms and mediums where the definition of design and designer will also change and evolve. The practice of design is not rooted in the discipline, but in the approach and process of designing and creating systems, ideas and solutions for a world with new challenges. Design will never cease to be a discipline as long as humans continue to create and stumble through new innovations and ideas. However, the practice and craft of design will continue to change and evolve in the future.

As we continue to progress into our future of uncertainty and unknowns within society, the impact of design continues to grow and become an important tool for building new ideas and communicating globally. Design within the context of this writing, is meant to explore the impact of design in the future and how designers can approach their work beyond their current discipline. Because the act and practice of design may evolve in the future, so we must also consider that the very act of design and being a designer must be looked upon, investigated, iterated upon and revised to accommodate a new landscape of design that is yet to come.

Design Practitioner vs. Design Thinker

As design tools through digital and print mediums become more accessible across the globe, we enter an era of design that allows many to explore what it means to be a design practitioner; that is to say, the techniques and time put into exploring the actual doing of design is greatly accessible. However, with all experienced designers, there is a strategy and thought process that develops over time. Years of exploration, failure, success and repeating this process around the actual doing of design manifests itself in the form of strategy, process and iterations on an individual and/or group level of involvement. Over time, designers begin to develop a heightened sense of design, recognize the positive parts of design and transform from being a practitioner of the craft to becoming recognized as a thought leader within the industry and organization.

In this new era of digital accessibility to many various design tools, designers who have been honing their craft for years (and even decades) should recognize their role in this fast moving atmosphere. Instead of becoming bitter about the onslaught of fly by night design shops and many unqualified people taking on design roles for their own projects and organizations; I believe it's important that we begin to recognize the clear delineation between a practitioner of design and a thought leader of design.

A practitioner is a worker.

The practitioner uses the tools necessary to work in the design medium required. In digital, these tools range from graphic design, prototyping, photo editing, front end development, video and motion design, among many other tools. The modern designer is multidisciplinary - not by choice, but by necessity of the industry, job market, and requirements of projects set forth by leadership who have recently begun to understand the value (economically) of good design.

A practitioner today has many responsibilities and is often regarded as a "unicorn" type to the organization, but, the reality is that these multidisciplinary designers are applying the foundational elements of design thinking across a wide range of tasks and mediums. These practitioners are examples of the true value of design thinking throughout multiple mediums, across organizations, and even in daily living. Design thinking is powerful and we are finally at the intersection of society where the value of this thinking will be an intrinsically important role within the advancement of commerce, culture and aesthetics both digital and physical.

Let us not confuse the value of design thinking with execution. They are different but possibly mutually beneficial. There are many design practitioners who are incredibly talented at their work but they lack the intuition or practical application of design thinking into their work. That is at no fault to them, but the oscillating balance between being a practitioner and a thinker is unbalanced. This is a dangerous space to operate. In my opinion, design will be moving towards the value of the ability to think as our tools for serving as a practitioner become more accessible and automated. Just as working in photoshop 15 years ago to edit pixel by pixel for retouching an image has become some from hours / days worth of work to a matter of seconds, being a practitioner in the execution is going to be more automated . Designers need to understand the balance and difference of a practitioner and thinker.

This balance and difference is the future of design and the design industry. Design must fully embrace the foundations of design in every aspect.

Without these foundations embraced and advocated at the highest level of designer, expectations of an end product is unrealistic is there is a lack of the foundations that have brought design to where it exists today. The execution within itself must rely on the balance between aesthetic, function, form, development, testing, feedback, experience, quantitative and qualitative data and aligning with the overall brand style and narrative. The metamodern designer takes all of this into account when working on a design. We cannot afford to have an unbalanced approach to our work with the role as designer in modern society.

As we move forward, we must not look at the design industry as having an identity crisis, but we must continue to advocate for the value of design, the importance of design fundamentals, communicating these values and providing true return on investment through every project. There is a great oscillation between being a practitioner within society and forging new paths with thinking and ideas and the future of design in society.

The Current State of Design

—

To be human is to create. I think the desire to create something deeply embedded within our DNA. Since the beginning of civilization, the discovery of fire and the invention of the wheel, humanity has been progressing into the unknown future of our existence with this primitive drive to explore, discover and create a world in which we envision the betterment of ourselves and those around us. Everything we experience in modern society has been a ripple effect of curiosity born out of the desire to create. To capture the essence of humanity. And in turn, resonate into the world we see today.

Design is a process by which we seek to solve challenges and discover solutions. Design is a broad term applied to many areas of the discipline and it's ubiquitousness today transcends traditional and classical ideas of design. We see the impact of design on micro and macro levels applied throughout current times. And the design approach is applied across many efforts in many industries across the world. It is not something strictly applied to designers who are seen as artists, architects or the unique and expressive cohorts of our times. Design exists within everything as the touch of humanity since the beginning of human time.

Everything we create exists within a designed approach. The refinement of that approach over time has led us to consider new ways to create, ideate, test, prototype and build new things at lightning speed.

Design became homogenized by a new era of "designers" who wanted to fit into the world in which they aspired to be like. Grasping onto the lifestyles of digital designers, we witnessed an influx of designers who were driven merely by ego and social status and not by that brooding internal desire to create new worlds born out of curiosity and a call to create culture.

So we watch as design trends become cyclical. Old designs mimicked and used as leverage to further someones career. The validity of design as seen by clients revolves around social status and how many followers someone has over the breadth and depth of their work and experience.

The narrative of design has shifted. It is misunderstood. The value of design is seen by companies as a "must have" but they don't really understand why. So they hire the most creative, eccentric, artistic person they can find who throws around the "designer" title.

The gap between business and design today misunderstands key concepts between their roles:

1. Design is not art.

2. Design is inherently integrated with business goals.

3. Designers of today will not operate like the designers of tomorrow.

4. Design processes of today will not be sustainable for design

needs of the future.

Classical Design

Classical Designers emerged from the Industrial Revolution, creating physical objects we use in our daily lives or experience throughout the physical world. Examples are Eames chairs, concert posters, IKEA furniture, a Louis Vuitton purse, clothing, everyday items found in your kitchen. The approach is to build something new to serve a way of living or to build upon references of past objects and make improvements.

"Which pertains to the design of objects we use in the physical world"

- John Maeda, Design in Tech Report

The Industrial Revolution brought on an entire movement of design - from steam powered engines, the lightbulb, electricity, power plants, manufacturing, and assembly lines.

Design Thinking

Design Thinking involves developing a framework(s) to understand a physical or digital challenge in the world and going utilizing tools and methods to uncover the challenges and create new solutions that can be tested, validated and iterated upon.

"Which pertains to how organizations learn how to collaborate and innovate using ideation methods" - John Maeda, Design in Tech Report

The first examples of design thinking emerged in the conception and creation of automobiles in the 60s and 70s.

The Evolution of Design in Enterprise by @libraiobabel outlines the

"Good definition of design thinking" sourced below:

Birth of traditional design for large corporations / corporate identity+image and product styling

1950s: GM's CEO makes the first executive position in design with Harley Earl elevated to VP.

1966: IBM Memo to IBM employees by CEO TJ Watson Jr. about the merging importance of design to the company

Birth of modern product design firms / from traditional design, to design of systems + services

1982: From 1982 Apple's design language begins to form with Frog and Harmut Esslinger's direction.

1991: David Kelley, Bill Moggridge, Mike Nutall join forces and change the course of design by co-founding IDEO

Birth of "Design Thinking" and design strategy / harnessing the creative problem solving skills of designers

2005: Hasso Plattner Institute of Design at Stanford starts. IDEO's Jane Fulton Suri publishes Thoughtless Acts? and brings design research to the foreground.

2008-09: Roger L. Martin describes design thinking at the CEO level with P&G's AG Laffley and his book on The Design of Business. (SAP and P&G were a few of the early executive adopters of Design Thinking.)

"Design Thinking" mainstreams as whole business strategy / re-contextualizing design, making B-Schools into D-Schools

2015-16: Phil Gilbert leads $100M bet to bring design back to IBM. Time Broen and Roger L. Martin open introductory issue for HBR on "The

Evolution of Design Thinking." Top 10 B-Schools all have student led design clubs.

2018: IBM Design open sources their Enterprise Design Thinking framework for all.

The Australian Government released a report on their studies of design in their country and stated this about design thinking:

"In the design profession and design education, research has focused on the forms of reasoning that underpin 'design thinking'. Dorst (2011) introduced the term 'frame creation' to refer to the formulation of a novel standpoint from which a problematic situation can be tackled. Research on design thinking emphasises the lifecycle of design skills and practices within an organizational context. Dorst argues that while there are underlying principles to design thinking that can be taught, "experienced designers develop up their own processes that work across projects within a firm or professional practice"."(IP Australia, "2014")

Computational Design

Utilizing the computer to aid in creating design decisions, we see the rise of software and programs that aid in these decision making processes. From templates, layouts, automation, and artificial intelligence in the digital design space. What was once left to the intuition and feeling of the designer is now being combined with computational efforts to speed up the process and mitigate design errors.

"Which pertains to any kind of creative activity that involves processors, memory, sensors, actuators, and the network." - John Maeda, *Design in Tech Report*

In the ArchDaily article *"5 Ways Computational Design Will Change The Way You Work"*, Michael Kilkelley describes computational design as the following:

"Computational design tools provide an easy way to harness the power of computation in a design process without having to learn how to write code. These tools let architects and designers create their own tools. Let's face it, each project we work on is unique with its own challenges. There's no one piece of software that can do everything we need it to. However, by creating our own tools, we can tailor our software to work for us." (Kilkelley, *"2016"*)

Kilkelley then describes the top 5 ways computational design will impact our work under the following categories.

- *Explore multiple design options*

- *Get under the hood and access your data*

- *Automate repetitive tasks*

- *Test what your design is REALLY doing*

- *Think algorithmically*

(Source: https://www.archdaily.com/785602/5-ways-computational-design-will-change-the-way-you-work)

Within these three areas of design (Classical, Design Thinking and Computational), we strive to create solutions among global, culture, emerging technology and workplace challenges. Design is simultaneously met with the subjective bias of the designer whom utilizes the innate facts of the challenge to discover and build a solution.

Though, this may not always be the case.

We can define designers as fitting into one of 3 categories. When we say we are a "Designer" it is often followed up with defining one of these categories. "I design posters and album art for musicians" or "I design for digital platforms" or "I design business strategy for global corporations". We define ourselves under one of three categories as if to segment our work.

However, I believe the future of design exists in a category beyond these three - and quite possibly merges all three of these together. As we progress into the future with automation, artificial intelligence, advanced technology, commoditization of creative fields and homogenized approaches to design solutions, I believe there is a 4th category that has yet to be defined and will emerge under an umbrella of culture, technology, design and creativity.

We cannot define this category in full until we recognize and define the role of the individual designer combined with the role of the individual designer related to the globalization of our work and also combined with the polarity of culture. All of this happening simultaneously to define a new breed of designer beyond the 3 traditionally defined categories.

(Note: Later on in this book, I coin the term "Ex-Designer" as a possible new category for designers in the future.)

I have personally worked as a designer within all three of these categories. I've had the opportunity to focus on highly visible projects and clients across each category. I've won awards, contributed to some really great projects and met some amazing people along the way. The approach to design across each category has a sentiment that resonates familiarity. But, the approach to each category is different and within each requiring a different approach. The path to discovering creative solutions and ideas is also different. It takes courage, bravery and thick skin to venture and explore each of these categories of design. The willingness to struggle and realize how much you don't know surfaces across each part.

Venturing into each area of design has helped me to become a better designer. As the landscape of design and the industry has changed dramatically over the past decade, exploring each category over the years has helped me to become an asset for my clients, to find connected solutions across possibilities and ideas.

The alternative is to stay in a single lane of design.

To be a strictly dedicated classical or traditional designer.

To only design UI / UX for digital.

To focus on developing strategies as a Design Manager for corporate teams.

I applaud those who can stick to a single path of design and adhere to it for decades. Building their own reputation as a "go-to" resource for a specific and nuanced need a client may have.

However, I find that this is limiting in certain aspects. First, you are at the whim of the client. You're value is determined by the ebb-and-flow of the need a client may have. You have honed your skills and approach to a specific niche relying on a client to come along and hire you for exactly the look and feel you have to offer.

The second limitation is that your work may become obsolete, either in demand by the market, or by the shear progress of technology. You become a "dinosaur".

My approach has been to diversify my design skills and portfolio in a way that I can take on work from all three categories - and be successful in those projects. Beyond the look and feel, which comes at the creative direction. Beyond the execution - the business goals and desired outcomes are incredibly important. We live in a world where clients expect speed over perfection. I do not strive to be perfect. If I do, I will never give the client what they need in a timely fashion.

I've worked on projects with millions of dollars of budgets stretching over multiple years. Building, designing and revising until it's "just perfect". However, the real perfection comes from the ability to understand you are not the expert. You are only a vessel to put things into motion and create something that has not yet existed. Honing your skills around traditional foundations of design is important to make initial decisions and good choices, but at the end of the day you can create a perfect end result that falls flat with your audience. This is where design needs to continuously shift from the categories of output to the intentions of what design actually is - approach and process.

But before we can look at the approach and process, we need to not only understand this history of design, but have an outlook of where design is headed.

Speculation.

I've speculated on culture many times in my past. I find that understanding culture helps to understand how we will move forward. Where are the trends? Where are the intentions? Politically? Socially? Economically? If we can shuffle all of these aside and dig deeper to understand the core desires and needs of humanity, we can start to see that piling a bunch of new technology, ideas, platforms and apps into the market is not going to solve the needs of people.

Everything is a circle.

Culture moves in circular waves. In my younger years, postmodernism was a rebuttal to the corporate monoliths of the 80s and 90s. Industry and corporate greed was beginning to grow in the United States. The counter-reaction to this from the younger generations emerged a movement of 90's grunge, rebellious culture around skateboarding, heavy metal, angsty baggy clothing and flannel. Those younger generations grew up to become the leaders, founders, executives, and workers of the currently existing companies. They may or may not have outgrown their younger ideals. If they didn't, they found their way into creative endeavors - many creative directors, designers, marketers, advertisers founded agencies that would compliment this ideal and carry into the future. Today we see that this postmodernist ideal that was once a rebuttal to the status quo has now become the status quo. And so, the younger generations look at the current landscape of culture in the way the younger generation did in the 80s and 90s and they are looking for new ways to identify, find their place in the world and add to the conversation. We can trace this backwards again to the 60s hippie movement. Where the rebuttal was against the suburban "Leave It To Beaver" ideal Americana of the 50s. And the 1950s emerges out of the desire to live a quality of life beyond the long struggle of the

Great Depression. And naturally the Great Depression was a cultural shift from reckless and irresponsible living of the Roaring Twenties.

Everything is a circle.

So, looking at this, we can see how generations emerge into being the drivers of culture and decisions. Their ideals formed in formative years and you either shed off the ideals and grow into someone else, or you use those ideals to propel yourself into a future version of you and your work.

Global impact of design.

Globally, design has become widely accessible through the digital medium. Access to software, digital tools, information and process has broken the barrier to entry from classical designers to forge ahead in new an innovative ways. This is both a blessing and curse. Design is utilized more now than ever as everyone has access to apps, tools and information on their mobile devices.

Design has been studied and systemized to drive commerce - from UX studies, best practices, templates, and sales funnels.

Globalization has seen the impact and benefits of design, whether society realizes it or not.

Design has influenced political movements. From the grassroots campaigns to raising more money than ever in history from the 2008 Obama presidential campaign (which I was a small part of). Design has provided a way for messaging and communication to reach specific and broad audiences while driving action in the form of assimilation, fund raising, protesting or providing a voice for those who generally go unheard. Design has drastically impacted politics within America and the the globe not just through the tools, but the effect and impact of those tools driving narratives, policy, cultural conversations and media attention.

Design has influenced the idea of our currency. The rise of cryptocurrency and BitCoin is a newly designed idea that seeks to solve a global challenge of monetary issues. The decentralization of currency is concept to socialize and create new power within the hierarchical structures of wealth within society.

Cultural impact of design.

Design is seen and felt culturally across many different facets. From the impact of consumer products, the rise of design in packaging has taken on new paradigms from the materials used, eco-conscious consumer products, the look and feel of the brand identity, colors and messaging to the way distribution for new products is designed within the business model.

Packaging design has been more prominent in trying to advance the technological side of packaging, the aerodynamics of design, to the minimalist approach as a call to nostalgia and the old days of craftsmanship and bespoke products.

Entertainment platforms are growing as a staple of our cultural influence. With the ability to watch and stream everything on demand, we find ourselves consuming more content than ever, exploring new ideas and gaining knowledge at lighting speed through platforms like Netflix, Amazon, Disney+, iTunes, podcasts, Spotify, Apple Music, Audible and an entire host of platforms designed to bring more content than we know what to do with in an immediately accessible format. These platforms did not exist within the general everyday lives of people 10 years ago. 20 years ago it was thought to be radical and high risk, while today we see the rise of entertainment studios fighting for survival, merging and crumbling because of these designed platforms that are changing how we consume media and ultimately how we perceive culture and our place within the world. All designed.

Political movements, beneath the surface, are designed. The intention, messaging, roadmap, policies, candidates and formats for narratives are all designed and disseminated across various platforms - digitally through documentaries, news outlets, emails, mobile apps, etc. All designed to inform, misinform, disseminate, activate or inspire us to form new beliefs or cement old beliefs. Politics are designed beyond the timelines we subscribe to them.

Social media has overtaken our lives. For better or worse. The design of these platforms have created an intention to connect, share and stay informed. However, we are starting to see the repercussions of these intentions as the leaders of these platforms do not have our best interests at heart compared to the desire for revenue, power and data.

We have a massive amount of access to information. There are no experts anymore because everyone is an expert. The ability to find and discover knowledge at our fingertips is both a blessing and curse.

Aesthetically we are bombarded more than ever with the impact of design. The efforts of visual design to market, promote, create lifestyle brands, utilize social media, capture attention, share, education and grow new ideas has never been greater.

Emerging technology impact of design.

The rapid speed of emerging tech forces design to move quickly, prototype, test, iterate and make improvements.

We are seeing a collective effort to design from different functions within a larger goal within artificial intelligence - both move rapidly to create and understand while being aware of the implications of the future impact this may have in our lives - yet we seem to be throwing our morals and judgements aside in pursuit of progress and innovation on this topic.

Autonomous vehicles are being developed and designed with the intention to create a better, safer and more efficient world where do not rely on the need of driving ourselves and operational of vehicles is not left to the impact of human error, but within the collective pursuit of a network of autonomous vehicles working seamlessly across roadways.

Battery powered cars, homes, buildings are being designed with the idea of taking digital approaches and classical approaches to design and merging them to create a more efficient, conscious, safer and energy efficient world through science, technology and design.

BitCoin and cryptocurrency is still in it's infancy, but we cannot ignore the impact this emerging technology may or may not have on our future of currency, globalization and commerce. Solar and wind power is still emerging.

Facial recognition technology is intended to make our world safer and more secure, yet we give up our privacy and rights of our identity in new and emerging ways. The implications of this are still being debated.

Biometrics being captured to ensure efficient health care, safety and security.

Workplace impact of design.

Redesigning workplace environments to feel differently for productivity, safety, inclusiveness, equality are all designed. Amidst the recent COVID-19 outbreak, we are seeing a shift in workplace culture and design of our workday by working remotely, collaborating digitally, taking meeting via video conferencing. Hiring and assembling teams and projects through digital mediums.

Global workplaces are now possible from the design of platforms like Zoom, Google, Skype, Slack and the all traditional email.

As the COVID-19 virus emerges as a global pandemic (I am writing this from my home in quarantine right now), we see a shift in business to adapt to these new challenges. A spike in in video conferencing, email and messaging has become a norm as we have the tools to adapt to the current pandemic. The unforeseen future will reveal how dependent and important these tools will be in our future.

In addition to these tools, I am personally fascinated with the idea of other tools to help us in business. Tools around emotional well-being, personal growth, mental health and the psychology of how we can design, adapt and consider the future. It is up to us to decide - but the compass we use to decide should be inspected and articulated and considered. Our tools for connectivity have never been greater. We can socialize, do business and create global economies because of the design of technology in our lives. However, the emptiness, isolation and loneliness is more prominent in our personal lives. The future challenges exist at an existential level where we may experience empty depths within our own purpose and meaning related to our individual self, our local impact and our individual place in a connected globalized world.

Our current world is experiencing the design of platforms, software, and seeing or subconsciously experiencing the impact of design in our everyday lives from a global, cultural, technology or workplace setting. Design is intertwined within our lives and as we progress more into a technological driven globalized world, the importance of design becomes not about what can we envision and create, but SHOULD we envision and create particulate things. Who governs this? Who funds these efforts? Who determines the implications and outcomes? Is there morality within design? If nature is natural and chaotic and free from morals, and humans have applied morality to the building of our society, should design and future efforts acknowledge the moral implications of our work as it becomes more intertwined and engrained with everyday lives of humans across the planet?

In my opinion, design has done a terrible job in it's infancy of taking on the responsibility and efforts of self-regulating the implications of morality within our work. From the diminishing value of output, to the lack of barrier to entry within our industry, to the over saturation of using design to drive political and social agendas for the sake of survival, relevancy and progress.

However, I question this deeply on many fronts. Whereas the current state of design is, in fact, in shambles. The creative agency model is broken, the drive for socialized design processes creates lackluster work, the lack of accountability has diminished our industry - all while the world needs responsible design met with thoughtful and considered approaches that are informed first by our approach to design itself, beyond and beneath the output. Yet, we see a flood of designers entering our field, those who do not have a background or experience in design taking our jobs or businesses bypassing the importance of our work.

But this is to no fault of anyone but the designers who have existed in this digital space for the past 20+ years, myself included. My hope for these writings is to share thinking about the intention of design, the roadmap of our future and how designers of the future must approach our work if we 1. want to relevant 2. want to impact the world at greater levels 3. have a seat at the table of larger global initiatives beyond the conversation of industrialization, profits and capitalism.

Top 10 emerging trends to have the biggest impact on design

1. *AI and machine learning*

2. *Augmented Reality*

3. *Virtual Reality*

4. *Behavior Tracking and modeling*

5. *3D printing*

6.   *Distributed teams and virtual workplace*

7.   *Democratization of design*

8.   *Crowdsourcing and open source*

9.   *Facial and voice recognition*

Source: Design Census AIGA, 2019

Uncertainty About the Future of Design

——

A s design tools have grown in access, there exists uncertainty about the future role of the designer. From Classical Design, Computational Design and Design Thinking, we envision a future where design leads, but the current leaders of industries do not see the value of design in the same regard. However, we can point to a few notes about the impact of design related to business, brands and commerce - though the data may not be as precise as desired, because design is a subjective output from objective thinking - hopefully. Most notably, The McKinsey Design Index does a good job of drawing correlation - but I am skeptical to their cherry-picking.

Whereas, Classical Design was born out of the view of a singular impression, computational design moves quickly with the intention to iterate and revise and design thinking is seen as a "must have" and not a specific practice within an organization. The lack of ROI or objective measurements leads those who do not design to see it as magic or unknown. They see the value of design from brands like Apple, Disney, or Tesla, and believe that if they create something aesthetically beautiful, it will sell and people will love it. However, this is flawed. Example - Microsoft Zoom was a well designed audio player that went obsolete.) The value of design exists beyond the aesthetic. Steve Jobs understood this. Apple understood this. Not all Designers understand this. Design is not about singular beauty, it is the ability to see beyond aesthetic, form and function and tap into the design of how we communicate our values and beliefs that are given life into our design.

In a 2018 Design in Tech Report open survey, 1219 samples from designers weighed in on the stereotypes designers experience in the modern work environment. The top stereotypes that non-designers believe to be true about designers is

"Designers make it pretty", "Designers can't lead teams", "Designers don't understand business", and "Designers only care about how it looks". (Maeda, "2018").

These stereotypes exist across agencies, in-house teams and startups across a wide spectrum of industries.

The design industry believes that socializing design, the process, and the work is enough of a belief system that should hopefully instill some mutated notion of values and beliefs within the product itself, yet it lacks the evangelistic notion that propelled Apple into a new stratosphere through capturing the beliefs about people and instilling them into the products. Design today is trying to do the inverse of this and then we wonder why 8 out of 10 startups fail. It's because the flaws of the design is not in the product, but the DNA that exists within the intention of that product in the first place.

There will never be another Steve Jobs. But what Steve Jobs understood is that humanity needed something greater than themselves. He actualized this belief through his products, his brand, his messaging, his existence.

Design exists in a place currently that is an attractive medium for those who desire to create. We exist within this unknown space. Where technology has given way to tools and resources and our best kept secrets. We are competing on price and a "race to the bottom". And simultaneously, we find it difficult to articulate the value of our work beyond ROI to business leaders and why they should pay us more for our work. It becomes a downtrodden place to live. But, I think there may be some answers in all of this.

Design is both subjective in execution and built in discovering facts to create new solutions. The problem currently exists in a world where the extreme differences in ideology points to the dismissal of facts if they do not align with an underlying individual or cultural bias. Therefore, the execution of the design becomes inherently bias in a way that may seem like it's doing good for the world, but it is ultimately contributing to the deterioration of the fabric of society.

For example, if we continue to silence, censor or ban the opinions of those whom we do not agree on a designed digital platform built on the values of freedom of speech, open source and self expression, what good is the effort of design if it has rooted itself within a political bias of subjective feelings versus freedom of speech in which it was designed does not agree with? Does this constitute silencing? This inherently changes the value of design. It diminishes the truth within design for the sake of pandering to bias narratives at the expense of going back on the values in which the pursuit of the design effort initially began.

Looking at you Twitter and Facebook.

The truth has slowly vanished from the design community. Truth being absolute rooted in fact to create and build a better future.

A bias truth without a foundation creates a fictional narrative and design direction that is not sustainable.

We witness this very unraveling at the polarity of extreme narratives being used through social media and network news. These narratives are designed not within facts, but within an underlying bias. The problem is that this approach to design creates a precedent that is not sustainable and diminishes the efforts and value of design in which it should be built upon discovery of facts, information and truth to solve challenges. If problems rise from a pursuit of truth within a design, then we must seek to discover a wider range of facts - or admit that we didn't uncover the truth to solve the challenge.

Globally, design faces many obstacles.

As our global world and connectivity increases, we adapt to new ways of doing business. Hiring remotely a collective group of designers from other countries who have garnered their skills from access to tools allows business owners and organizations to hire designers for a fraction of the cost.

The commoditization of design has diminished the value and price at which we were once hired for, only to have business owners and investors look elsewhere for cheaper work because the access to design and tools have become widely accessible.

We have seen the global effect of design create a diminishing return on opportunities and the ability to hire designer's at the cheapest costs.

New design platforms exist to hire designers as a commodity, versus the value that we intrinsically bring with our work and experience. If hiring strictly on past portfolio is the only metric, designers wouldn't need to sell themselves continuously beyond their past performance. But we do, and that translates to the potential client bidding on the notion of "how cheap can you do this for us?".

We find ourselves competing globally against other designers across multiple continents for a design job that requires deep thinking, experience and a nuanced approach to discover and design the best possible solution. Yet, business owners want what they want and they will gladly pay a fraction of the price many times over until they find a designer who will meet their every need and request.

This globalization has created opportunity to connect globally, but we are experiencing a greater sense of depression and loneliness through these digital channels. Compounded on top of the diminishing industry within design, this creates future uncertainty about the impact and relevance of design as a place of leadership, influence and impact.

Compounded on top of the design industry and perception of our value, as humans, we face uncertainty related to global economics, politics, distribution of goods and services, natural disasters, pandemics, outbreaks, climate change impact, corporate and global economical power structures, technology implemented at mass scale (via commerce and physical checkout systems), biometrics, data privacy, 3d printing, direct to consumer models, and the downfall of brick and mortar business.

All of these examples are shifting dramatically, unknown, or pose a risk to stability.

Culturally, design now fast follows current trends - via the invention of a "new" app that competes with already existing apps in a dominated market space, aesthetically mimicking the look of brand identity or marketing campaigns in entertainment, consumer goods or services. Smaller startups are chasing influential brands for identity, marketing, design and visual. We see a constant remix and recycling of ideas as a means to compete or try to be different at the cost of informing design decisions from other successful companies.

There is a clash within society between modern and postmodern ideals. Where the hierarchy of structure is being dismantled from cultural narratives of western civilization for the pursuit of equality beyond opportunity. The design of society that created the modern world is being destroyed with no clear direction of what happens after the destruction. Meanwhile, those who choose to preserve the old-world design models in society are harboring the power and control as a survival mechanism. These ideals have driven a wedge within business and design. Whereas the majority of the design culture embraces the postmodernist ideals, yet takes a paycheck (happily) from the business owners who have built a structure, system and model from the industrialized ideals of the Modernist's world. And the designers (in the majority) stand upon the ideals of postmodernism in an empty virtue of disrupting culture while accepting payment from the ideals in which they so profoundly despise.

We see extreme political activism happening. A polarizing political system that permeates culture at every turn. The narrative threads are woven into the subtle pieces of design, messaging, articles and business from those who instill these beliefs covertly or subconsciously. Designers must pick a side and stand for something greater than their work to implore meaning and purpose - so design chooses politics... because it's easy.

Politically driven narratives subtly infused within the (sub)conscious efforts of designers inform the approach and intention behind the brand, identity, visual look and feel to create equity beyond equality of opportunity.

Narcissism via social media.

The prominence of social media in our world has created a self-centered and narcissistic worldview. We do things in order to share, to be admired, to gain followers, to capture likes, to hold attention. The narcissism is the desire to be like a celebrity, or pursue fame and relevancy as the access to social media is open to everyone. And this creates a platform in which the structural ideals are left to human instinct and it has brought out the worst of ourselves. We post to share, but deep down we desire to be loved, admired and revered. We post on others to bring them down, or lift them up in hopes that others will shape their views and opinions accordingly. The destruction of the social fabric of society has been left up to the reckless approach of social media - designed without any intention other than to socialize a platform of connection and accessibility.

With this consecutiveness, we gather insights into others lives and subconsciously create a social hierarchy (actualized by followers and likes) within a platform built and supported by those who seek to dismantle the structures and hierarchies by way of postmodernism. Do you see the hypocrisy within this?

So we have an intention of design, and industry of design led by those who value design, but not for the approach and intention that was greatly exemplified by the designers who built Rome, or considered the Egyptian pyramids, or built high-rises of New York City, or led Henry Ford to build an automobile, or the Wright Brothers to continuously and tireless pursue the idea of flight.

The fabrics of those societies where much different, and I would suggest that their morality and design was for the betterment of man, not for the destruction of culture and society. When the early Steve Jobs or Bill Gates set out to disrupt the computer industry, they saw it as an opportunity to create an amazing world by way of computers and connectivity. The IBM and Xerox's of the world were dominated by stale corporate business leaders who lacked vision with the power of computing. Jobs and Gates saw an opportunity.

Today, those tools are now being used as a means of cultural influence and driving narrative - whereas the platforms that exist, and are designed, are created with the intention to disrupt, not to improve our lives, but to dismantle.

How can I say this with such certainty?

Because these companies such as Facebook, Twitter, Instagram and other social media platforms are incredibly aware of their impact and influence - there is more negative than positive examples in the world, and instead of course correcting and evaluating their deeper values of their existence, they continue to push forward at the expense of the user, data and revenue. They do not have our best intentions at heart. Maybe they did at one time, but the very thing that the value systems of those who work at these companies profess to speak out against, is the same thing fueling their operation and company vision. Money - at the cost of your well being. So they sell you on yourself. You are the product. And the more you can buy into your own narcissism, the more addicted you become to their platform. And the more addicted you are to their platform, the more money they make from you both as a product and a consumer.

Fast following trends, chasing influential brands, remixing and recycling ideas, clash of modern and postmodern ideals, extreme political activism, narcissism via social media, misunderstandings of branding, misunderstanding of design, streaming platforms and entertainment, brands are taking a political and social position, celebrities and entertainers are being a voice of global change, politicians are focused on being celebrity personas.

Will AI replace design? Will data and automation replace design? Will access to new and free design tools continue to diminish our work and role?

Will emerging tech replace us? Will emerging tech create an even lower barrier to entry for anyone to design? How will viruses and pandemics effect our work in the future? How will corporate culture change? How can design effect and impact depression and mental health? Do we have the proper tools for working remote? How long will it take to naturalize the digital workplace and work-from-home?

The future will be impacted by direct to consumer, social media, biometrics, data privacy, streaming platforms, cloud computing, startups, tech companies, and facial recognition.

Design does not have a prominent seat at the executive level.

Design has struggled to be validated or quantified with its impact beyond the execution of the work.

Design Has Become A Commodity

—

The commodification of design is a result of the failures within the design and creative industries. Beyond the trade, skill, practice and discipline of design, the industry is touted as a construct of social hierarchy within the design and creative communities themselves. The ideological structures are formed around groupthink that you first, must subscribe to the values of the group and second must display these values within your work in order to maintain relevance or climb the social hierarchy within the design and creative fields. From here, you may be recognized by the community and therefore garner the accolades, attention and recognition for your work. The social structures are both determined by the old-world thinking and values of design beyond design itself. It is rooted within the values of the individuals who have served as the gate-keepers of the design and creative fields.

Furthermore, new opportunities for designers and creatives have emerged and the value placed on those individuals who have set out to garner value through their offerings are validated within the design and creative communities ONLY IF they meet the criteria of the group first and foremost. This idea rests in the notion that the designer must exist within a liberal political belief. They must use their design as a tool to fight for ideals or fight against ideals that do not align with the groupthink as a collective. They must blend in and homogenize their work to the likes of the group for self validation, group validation and to garner new work and opportunities not based on their skillset, but on the ability to rise within the social heirarchies of creative fields to attract the attention of those who might become their client based on the premise that they themselves have not only become proficient in the field of design, but they have fully taken on the expected identity of a modern-day creative.

I have observed for years the slow crumbling and dismantling of the creative community by placing value on the identity of the individual by subscribing fully to the ideals and communal thinking guided by gate-keepers. And those gatekeepers are leveraging their careers by standing on the intersections of their identity beyond the actual work.

Promoting the political rhetoric where the discussion around design is somehow infused with political leanings that align with progressive ideals, as if, those ideals are somewhat more noble and justified in design over any other alternative belief. To question this premise is to become non-hirable, uncreative and unworthy of being a part of the design com-munity.

The gatekeepers leverage a political narrative as a way to justify their own path to "design success" and maintain their own sense of self-worth and power within the social hierarchy of the design community. The dismantling and disruption they chose to pursue in the 90's and 2000's has paved a way for their own success and career path; giving them a platform to speak to their own beliefs outside any relevance to the practice of design.

My problem with this is that design should be non-partisan and apolitical. Design is about identifying the truth of the challenge and discovering the truth of a solution beyond political ideology or rhetoric in which a designer "must" align in order to assume he or she can have any impact in the world. This thinking creates an echo chamber within the design industry. We then get communities of creative efforts rooted in Los Angeles, Silicon Valley, Seattle and New York. Assuming that the only valuable thinkers and minds have somehow accepted that, in order to succeed, you must be a progressive liberal leaning person to make impactful and valuable design.

The young designers and followers of design iconoclasts either subscribe and echo these sentiments or risk being ostracized by their community.

The problem here is not that the ideals and topics they are discussing is invalid. The problem is that they are using these topics to leverage the validity of their voice in design, beyond the work. They have garnered attention and if you disagree with their political and social beliefs, you are ostracized from the group. If you buy into their beliefs and agree, you give up your ability to be an individual designer.

It's a tempting path. Where the validity of design is built on the notion of followers, influence and ability to be a leading voice in the room. However, these voices are a homogenized predictable echo-chamber of values and ideals within the creative industry that has created a postmodern conversation of boring and predictable work rooted in disruption, sex appeal, provocative ideas and pushing boundaries for the sake of seeking attention.

My opinions about design and creativity are built from the experience of past work and within various design and creative communities. From working in-house at global brands, agencies, startups, creative communities.

After watching the validity of design and creativity being determined beyond the work and built upon the groupthink narratives that drive the community - I began to question my own values. Over time, the values and hierarchical structures within the creative communities felt like I was not myself. The individual is only worth their creative approach, as long as their other values aligned with the group. The more your values intersected within ideologies, the more you would be accepted and validated for your work, thus resulting in more notoriety.

In addition, the commodification of design is a result of leadership within organizations lacking the usefulness of design and the work of designers. In the 2018 Design in Tech Report open survey, 1219 samples identified the core problems designers face from leadership in their organizations.

"Be clear about the business problem", "Advocate for the user", "Allow for failure" and "Ask questions to build empathy"(Maeda, "2018")

Designers are lacking in leadership where design exists. To improve possible outcomes, designers have stressed the need for these ideas to be included in their work. The alternative results in design becoming a commodity and misunderstood and under-utilized.

However, design is seeking to evolve and shift out from this commodification. The value of design has been underutilized in recent years and the growing sentiment among designers is clear. Models of design processes, workplace culture, design ethics and continuing the dialogue around design has further evolved in recent years.

Evidence has begun to emerge related to processes, models, data and research showing the impact that design has beyond current expectations. Where the ROI of design is seen as a correlation between companies who succeed and the models in which they utilize design to outperform expectations and their competitors.

InVision's "Five Levels of Design Maturity"

InVision surveyed 2,200 design professionals to provide insight into companies utilizing design and the level of maturity in which they progress. (Source: @invisionapp: Design Maturity Model)

1. Producers 41% - Design is what happens on screen

"At this level, organizations make early attempts to create efficiency and consistent story though visual identity guidelines but neglect processes, collaboration and advanced tools."

(Source: @invisionapp: Design Maturity Model)

Most designers and small agencies exist at this level. They try to implement visual guidelines and standards with a focus on aesthetic, but fail to progress at the maturity of the following steps. This is both at the maturity of the designer and also the maturity of the organization and leadership.

2. Connectors 21% - The workplace becomes a workshop

"User research, user stories, usability testing, and personas are also more prevalent. Overall, there's more talk of design in the air - from executives who espouse its importance to the employees who express more interest and empathy for customers."

(Source: @invisionapp: Design Maturity Model)

This level of design becomes a progression of understanding the value of design and how research can impact the direction moving forward. Utilizing data and research to make informed decisions to mitigate risk for bigger challenges and higher stakes in projects.

3. Architects 21% - Design is a scalable operation

"They have shared ownership, role clarity, joint accountability, and more documentation of their now more substantial design practices. This enables design to support complex ecosystems while integrating with complex internal operating structures."

(Source: @invisionapp: Design Maturity Model)

As the results from research, data and testing had proven out successful outcomes, the organization decides to implement more design focused initiatives through structures within the organization infused across the DNA of various disciplines.

4.Scientists 12% - Design is powered by hypothesis

"They have sophisticated practices for analytics, experimentation, recruiting for user research, and monitoring and measuring the success of specific efforts. They also have the beginnings of a design

strategy practice and vision development."

(Source: @invisionapp: Design Maturity Model)

This maturity level recognizes that the impact of design is built into utilizing deep analytics and research to understand the challenges at depth before diagnosing solutions. My business in Neon Wilderness is built from this foundation.

5. Visionaries 5% - Design means business

"Design brings a unique lens to strategy thought exploratory user research techniques, trends and foresight research that assesses product market fit, and the delivery of unified cross-platform strategies.

(Source: @invisionapp: Design Maturity Model)

This approach is essential to the future of design. In my work, I have developed a proprietary patent-pending process where I merge massive amounts of data to build and deliver strategies for business, brands and design solutions across digital and physical mediums. The focus of my work (and small parts of this book) is focused on moving from each level of maturity throughout my career. I appreciate that InVision has broken this maturity model down into these steps. In my opinion, you must start at maturity level one and commit to the journey of design to reach maturity level five.

McKinsey's Design Index

The McKinsey Design Index looks at research and data of top performing companies across multiple sectors and evaluates their design impact within the business and on their product or service. Tracking the progress of 300 publicly traded companies over 5 years with two million pieces of financial data and recorded 100,000 design actions reveals the greatest correlation with improved financial performance across design themes. (McKinsey, "2018")

1. Companies with top quartile McKinsey Design Index scores outperformed industry-benchmark growth by as much as two to one. (McKinsey, "2018")

2. Higher McKinsey Design Index scores correlated with higher revue growth and, for the top quartile, higher returns to shareholders. (McKinsey, "2018")

3. The financial outperformance of top-quartile companies holds true across the three industries studied.(McKinsey, "2018")

Research yielded several striking findings:

"We found a strong correlation between high MDI scores and superior business performance. Top-quartile MDI scorers increased their revenues and total returns to shareholders (TRS) substantially faster than their industry counterparts did over a five-year period—32 percentage points higher revenue growth and 56 percentage points

higher TRS growth for the period as a whole.

The results held true in all three of the industries we looked at: medical technology, consumer goods, and retail banking. This suggests that good design matters whether your company focuses on physical goods, digital products, services, or some combination of these." (McKinsey, "2018")

The Value of Design reflected across these top performing companies is distilled down to 4 models. *Analytical Leadership, Cross-Functional talent, Continuous iteration, User Experience (McKinsey, "2018")*

"Companies that tackle these four priorities boost their odds of becoming more creative organizations that consistently design great products and services. For companies that make it into the top quartile of MDI scorers, the prizes are as rich as doubling their revenue growth and shareholder returns over those of their industry counterparts." (McKinsey, "2018")

Design in Tech Report

The past few years, John Maeda has put out a Design in Tech Report focusing on the current trends within design and the predictions of where design is headed based on research, surveys and analysis.

Key takeaways from these reports are the following:

• *There are three kinds of design. Classical Design, Design Thinking, and Computational Design.*

• In the last 12 months there were 19 acquisitions of creative agencies and companies.

• The value of design is in relation to the other parts of a company's operations.

• Alone and isolated within a company, design is a microworld of aesthetic high-fives.

• Scaling design at the speed of Moore's Law is not possible.

• Scaling design IS possible at a slower-thandesirable velocity.

• Inclusive design has achieved broad acceptance among designers.

• For non-designers, inclusive design can be a harder idea to sell.

• There's fear about AI's future impact, but there's creative hope out there too. Yes we can.

(Source: Design in Tech Report, 2019, Maeda, J.)

In 2019, Design Census (design census.org) shows results from a survey of 9,429 people that a majority of designers have 5-9 years of experience and work mostly in digital products, advertising and marketing industries. Their income is between $50,000-$79,000 per year. Most feel happy but not completely satisfied with their role. Assumptions made here is the role in which they work in the organization, their contribution to the strategic approach to their work or the pay in which they make for the work. (Designcensus.org, "2019")

Average industry growth for graphic designers from 2015-2020 has seen a -0.8% growth rate. (IBISWorld, "2020") Where the assumption is that the tools and resources for companies to create their own graphic design in house has increased and the need for a designer with a select skillset has diminished in demand. Graphic design employs 155,816 people with a market size of $13B. As access to design tools increase, the market size will decrease to save and cut costs for hiring designers. We have seen the decline over the past 5 years.

In addition, IBISWorld states *"Demand for the Graphic Designers industry is expected to decline in 2020 due to a decrease in total advertising spending from businesses." (IBISWorld, "2020")*

From a competitive perspective within the industry, we see data showing that design agencies and companies are competing on price over the value of the impact they offer. In addition to the decline in demand for designers, the competitive pricing also creates decline in the industry overall.

"Regional economic activity drives demand, because most graphic design firms are small and work locally. The profitability of individual companies depends on accurate bidding, timely delivery of projects, and a steady volume of work. Large companies have advantages in marketing and sales, breadth of services, delivery of complex projects, and supporting ongoing contracts. Small companies can compete effectively by responding more quickly, adopting new trends, and specializing by services or markets. The US industry is highly fragmented: the

50 largest companies account for less than 15% of revenue." (Dun & Bradstreet, "2020")

There becomes a constant threat of new entrants into the design industry. Diminishing returns are due to bargaining power of buyers and bargaining power of other sellers. The added threat of substitute products or services creates a pattern where design has become a commodity.

University of Salford, Manchester UK states the following in their Design 2020 Report:

"In line with the shift of the UK economy, there is a growing recognition that through the effective integration of design - linking creativity and innovation, and shaping ideas to become practical and attractive propositions for users or customers (Cox, 2005) - companies are more likely to be innovative, become more competitive, increase their profits and boost their performance. This is confirmed by research (Design Council, 2006) in which design is seen as a key driver of business growth and competitiveness. However, it is also recognized that many companies, especially UK-based SMEs, are missing the huge opportunity that design and creativity can offer, that SMEs typically lack aspiration, are unable to see the relevance of design, often lack the skills and don't know where to turn to engage with the design industry (The Work Foundation, 2007). It is apparent that UK industry as a whole has to find ways in which it could increasingly use design to add value to its products and services in order to differentiate them in highly competitive markets. These issues rather

than being less important in the current economic climate are in fact more important. To operate in the future our design knowledge and skills will be one of the means of moving out of recession." (University of Salford, "2020")

The pattern for design has revealed that the classical and traditional designers are in less demand and therefore become more specialized as the growth of demand for technology and digital designers is still needed. However, as more access to tools, the decline of designers are needed, and substituted products and services becoming automated and available creates a threat for the future of digital design as much as it has had an impact on classical print design.

"The Technology and Interactive Design industries are more common with people who have less than ten years of experience, while people who have twenty or more years of experience are more likely to be in the Print and Advertising industries. These patterns reveal how job opportunities in the tech sector are continuing to grow, while older industries like print are perhaps becoming more limited or specialized." (Sosolimited, "2017")

Commodification of design has been happening and data supports this. And this commodification seems to contribute to a "race to the bottom" mentality that threatens the design industry as a whole because of the unfocused offerings the client wants to push onto consumers with new designed products or services. Design becomes an order taker to stay in business and the client is not tapping into the added value design can have beyond the output of the work.

"The challenge isn't new in our industry and the solution seems so simple, and yet very few are leveraging it. As organizations look to innovate or renovate their brands or offerings they continue to look within at what the company can make, what they have capacity for, or what a customer has asked for. They may even look to the category, competition or adjacent categories playing the "me too" game, creating products that lack a meaningful point of difference for consumers. Compounding the problem is the prevalence of designers seeking inspiration from the category (or the likes of Pinterest) rather than watching people and behaviours, and listening to the consumer aspiration, translating those insights into big ideas." (Roberts, M. RGD, "2017")

The medium contributed to the message. The medium related to the industry and digital has changed. There is diminishing returns as a designer and I am thinking about the next level of design. There is pretense to design. A church, a road system, a theatre, an orchestra house. The radio. Tv. The escape. The phone and digital has become a portal to drive business, advertiser and constant selling - it used to be a place of curiosity and inspiration and experience or discovery. The journey of digital design has changed to a commoditized expenses for driving business. But design is greater and has informed the progress of humanity in different forms. It has evolved during different time periods and revolutions - industrial revolution. Design today is a last stop for business to continue churning but the fulfillment in the work is not what drove designers to be stuck within their situation.

As the commodification of the industry continues, designers need to find ways to pivot and adjust to the fast-changing landscape that technology has created (and will continue to drive) in terms of opportunities for design and jobs within digital innovations. Design must find new ways to advocate for the value beyond the work. To encompass the strategy, process and overall impact beyond the aesthetic of design.

"In 1959, design was largely recognized as a noun, synonymous with style. Postwar consumption and the growth of the American middle class fueled the notion that design stimulated repeat consumption and accompanied the peak of planned obsolescence. Today, design, increasingly understood as a verb, is core to the value proposition and often accompanies disruption. With our focus moving from designing artifacts and products to designing experiences, we have gone from designing "how it looks" to designing "how it works."(IIT Institute of Design, "2020")

Discovering
Metamodernism

—

In order to define and articulate the concept of metamodernism and how it relates to design, I believe it is important to outline my view of culture by looking at the past to understand where we are today. This understanding will give light into how I see the cultural path of humanity's future along with how we can consider the role of design - not justice as a designer - but for humanity to utilize design to make new understandings of our world, to discover new solutions in our rapidly changing world and to approach design as a practice beyond the modernist or post-modern approaches that design has existed within.

I believe these ideas form a foundation of my thinking about how design, creativity, thinking and new ideas can shape our future. If we don't recognize this, we risk serious implications of a constant pull between extreme cultural polarities that are meant to divide, disrupt, confuse and distort reality. Beyond this exists true individual freedom. As designers, I believe it is our job to be hyper aware of these cultural movements and use this information for good and for a better future for humanity. I deeply fear the path we are headed currently. The rising status quo of post-modernism combined with the extreme polarities within culture are tools for the powerful and the elites to divide and confuse in order to build a paradigm of control, enslavement and a path toward an Orwellian existence for mankind. Maybe Aldous Huxley and George Orwell weren't so far off. Maybe media and entertainment are priming us for a bit so distant reality of a dystopian future. If we can use design through the lens of metamodernism to awaken humanity and build a strong internal sense of self purpose and meaning, there is hope for a future where freedom can exist for all humanity. Design plays an integral part in this and it begins with us, right now.

Metamodernism has been an exploration of thoughts, work, art, design and music in my life. A framework to explore ideas and express them in various forms. Keeping a close eye on culture and finding various examples that seemingly emerge in unexpected places. Over that time, I have been writing and unpacking my own thoughts around metamodernism and what it means to me. The application of this feeling in the current cultural landscape has revealed new truths to me and shifted my perceptions around cultural ideas and narratives. I think it has provided a framework of feeling and understanding in which I could make sense of the individual self related to the greater good of a globally connected world. Through this, I began exploring this idea through the lens of design. While I don't think I have everything figured out, I hope that my first explorations unpacked in this writing will help to inspire other designers or those who work in brand and business to make sense of the future of our cultural world.

The writings in this work seek to express the views of culture from a modern, postmodern and metamodern lens in which I then try to unpack my view of metamodernism from a designer's perspective. I try and break down the sensibility, ideas, emotions and thoughts about the future of design and a designer's role within a metamodern world. From my own perspective, these writings serve as self-examination of the understandings I have learned over the past 7 years of looking at culture and design from a lens of the active and observant designer - both from the view of the self, and within the design industry. My goal is to explore these ideas and offer up the truths in which I have discovered related to the pendulum oscillating observations and feelings within culture, and therefore, how to do those feelings translate to future work of design. I then try to unpack what it means and what it might look like to exist as a designer within the future context of a cultural feeling that exists between both modernism and post-modernism. How does design exists within both without getting lost within the commitment to one polarity or the other? My initial belief here, as I have worked through and tried to make sense of this for myself, is that the designer, as aware of their own design, must also choose to be aware of the self within the context of society and simultaneously aware of the collective society as a whole in order to design within the oscillation and create new works emerging from a new sensibility.

Metamodernism is a way to describe a structure of feelings based on the current cultural and sociological conditions of society. Metamodernism is not a belief system in of itself. It is meant to describe and then further articulate the sense of feeling that exists between the polarities of both modernism (sincerity) and post-modernism (irony) that we are succumbed and conditioned to among the many aspects and narratives of the current modern world.

Metamodernism is not a way to define or redefine belief systems, but to recognize the extreme polarities of beliefs about the world and discover the truth within the polarities. And within the polarities, there exists truth beneath. The world is complicated and complex. It is not as easy as to subscribe to a set of ideologies in the extreme and write off or discredit the ideologies of another. However, the ability to think and unpack the ideas and make sense about the validity of those ideas goes beyond the affirmations you provide to yourself or gain from the group in which you seek to belong.

Metamodernism is saying and recognizing that the pendulum of ideals and feelings swing back and forth and we choose to exist on one side or the other. However, by choosing an extreme rooted in either modernism or post-modernism we are doing a disservice to ourselves and to our community by steering clear of the uncomfortable tension where Metamodernism explores the ability to exist between the two polarities. Within the weightlessness of understanding "both/and" outside of "either/or". That you can have both understanding and beliefs that validate from modernism and post-modernism because beyond the acceptance of the groupthink mindset, you have chosen to exist within the tension of both, unpack these ideals, observe them and understand and define a set of truths for yourself beyond the expectations a communal set of ideologies.

If we, as designers and creatives, truly believe that we are leading culture, humanity and creating a better future - we should recognize that it is our responsibility to step outside of the ideologies that trap us, that we should have the courage to define for ourselves, without fear of being ostracized, to define what the future looks like beyond a set of ideologies.

Because the design and creative communities have chosen to take a path of ideological stance's to validate or invalidate the work of the individual beyond the measurement of success and impact of the work, they have simultaneously commodified their own industries. The reason that design has lost of sense importance to clients, to leadership and to those potential clients is because the design and creative community has allowed those who sit at the top of the social dominance hierarchy speak for the rest of design beyond the work and aligning the validity of design and creativity to be inherently rooted in ideologies. They have ultimately cut off 50% of the American population by an authoritative stance of creative work and ostracizing themselves from finding new work because they would rather stand and die on a hill of broken post-modern narratives instead of focusing on the work. At every opportunity design leaders choose to make a political or cultural statement not to change anything, but to fit into the creative community in hopes that their own sense of self-importance will be recognized enough that it may garner new work for themselves. All while standing on the shoulders of the community who continues to support these beliefs and narratives. And dare I say anything, or have an opinion or think for myself. Dare I even believe that I speak up and speak as a creative with individual opinions that may or may not exist outside the expected narrative of these so-called creatives.

I believe that sharing these ideas have helped me unpack meaning and purpose for myself. The effort within itself poses an exercise that left me feeling both attached and detached from my work. Trying to discover truth, share and articulate without finding myself being too attached to the emotions and feelings behind them. In addition, I could have flooded these writings with evidence, and data and research and spent another 5 years capturing all of the proof that went along with validating or invalidating my perspectives. However, in the spirit of metamodernism, I hope that these writings will simultaneously connect you to a sense of self, while connecting to my own sense of self and emerge some form of understanding beyond your own existence in the ways in which these thoughts and writings have emerged new sensibilities about myself related to meaning and purpose.

Modernism

"Modernism is both a philosophical movement and an art movement

that arose from broad transformations in Western society during the late 19th and early 20th centuries. The movement reflected a desire for the creation of new forms of art, religion, philosophy, and social organization which reflected the newly emerging industrial world, including features such as urbanization, new technologies, and war. Artists attempted to depart from traditional forms of art, which they considered outdated or obsolete. The poet Ezra Pound's 1934 injunction to "Make it new!" was the touchstone of the movement's approach." - ("Modernism", 2020)

These new modes of expression were derivative of the building of a better society. For the "dignity of man". We observe the rise of the industrial revolution, massive innovation, infrastructure and the the pursuit of building a more advanced society. In art and literature, this took on pursuit of creating new forms of expression of this industrial world and making sense of the future of society and humanity. The arts made a conscious break from traditional forms of art - classical, neoclassical, etc. and sought to define new ways of meaning that complimented the industrialization of society.

This departure from Enlightenment lead society into new industrialized ways of thinking about humanity. From building roads, bridges, manufacturing and lifting up the state of humanity from darker times. Modernism was meant to drive culture through the lens of "dignity of man" where all come together and work towards a greater building of society. The arts, culture and economics of the time reflected in these efforts. Modernism was a new outlook from beyond the perspective of the self and into a perspective of the whole. Generated through a sincere attempt of creating a better world for the society.

"The Modernist impulse is fueled in various literatures by industrial-
ization and urbanization and by the search for an authentic response
to a much-changed world. Although prewar works by Henry James,
Joseph Conrad, and other writers are considered Modernist, Mod-
ernism as a literary movement is typically associated with the period
after World War I. The enormity of the war had undermined human-
kind's faith in the foundations of Western society and culture, and
postwar Modernist literature reflected a sense of disillusionment and
fragmentation. A primary theme of T.S. Eliot's long poem The Waste
Land (1922), a seminal Modernist work, is the search for redemption
and renewal in a sterile and spiritually empty landscape. With its
fragmentary images and obscure allusions, the poem is typical of
Modernism in requiring the reader to take an active role in interpret-
ing the text." (Kuiper)

This desire to build and construct and make something greater beyond
the self was a cleansing, a renewal, a redemption from the ugly parts of
society past.

"In an era characterized by industrialization, rapid social change,
and advances in science and the social sciences (e.g., Freudian
theory), Modernists felt a growing alienation incompatible with Vic-
torian morality, optimism, and convention. New ideas in psychology,
philosophy, and political theory kindled a search for new modes of
expression." - (Kuiper)

The idea of utilizing line, form and color translated to how those beyond painting could influence society. Brutalism in architecture focused on function and form, music became less grandiose and emerges more simple styles of music emerging blues, jazz, rock within the early 1900s. Fashion broke away from the Victorian and French influences. Things became more about the structure and less about the ornate.

Instead of forcing a representation through an artists viewpoint, the intention was to create forms in which the interpretation could be held up and determined by the masses and also by the individual.

"By the beginning of the 20th century, architects also had increasingly abandoned past styles and conventions in favour of a form of architecture based on essential functional concerns. They were helped by advances in building technologies such as the steel frame and the curtain wall. In the period after World War I these tendencies became codified as the International style, which utilized simple geometric shapes and unadorned facades and which abandoned any use of historical reference; the steel-and-glass buildings of Ludwig Mies van der Rohe and Le Corbusier embodied this style. In the mid-to-late 20th century this style manifested itself in clean-lined, unadorned glass skyscrapers and mass housing projects." (Kuiper)

Evidence of Modernism - "Sincerity"

Modernism arose as both a philosophical movement and an art movement. The growth began around the late 19th and 20th centuries with the rise of the industrial revolution. This movement began as a progression of society to build and construct for the betterment of man. The surge and growth of cities, construction of buildings, institutions, skyscrapers, transportation and systems designed for society to give man meaning and building a new construct of society throughout progress.

As a form of philosophical thought, modernism is defined by self-consciousness and awareness to create newness within society. A sincere approach to build better solution for society as a whole. Modernist look at every aspect of the lie existence and evaluate opportunities to create progress and better outcomes.

According to Roger Griffin, modernism can be defined in a maximalist vision as a broad cultural, social, or political initiative, sustained by the ethos of "the temporality of the new". Modernism sought to restore, Griffin writes, a "sense of sublime order and purpose to the contemporary world, thereby counteracting the (perceived) erosion of an overarching 'nomos', or 'sacred canopy', under the fragmenting and secularizing impact of modernity."

Examples of modernism throughout history are found during the French Revolution, the Enlightenment era, the Scientific Revolution, the idea of building "the Dignity of Man", and an overarching sentiment about the story of progress through societal structures, systems and ideals. Much of the modern western world was built through the lens of modernists.

This merging of consumer and high versions of Modernist culture led to a radical transformation of the meaning of "Modernism". First, it implied that a movement based on the rejection of tradition had become a tradition of its own. Second, it demonstrated that the distinction between elite Modernist and mass consumerist culture had lost its precision. Some writers declared that modernism had become so institutionalized that it was now "post avant-garde", indicating that it had lost its power as a revolutionary movement. Many have interpreted this transformation as the beginning of the phase that became known as postmodernism.

For others, such as art critic Robert Hughes, postmodernism represents an extension of modernism.

"In the visual arts the roots of Modernism are often traced back to painter Édouard Manet, who, beginning in the 1860s, broke away from inherited notions of perspective, modeling, and subject matter. The avant-garde movements that followed—including Impressionism, Post-Impressionism, Cubism, Futurism, Expressionism, Constructivism, de Stijl, and Abstract Expressionism—are generally defined as Modernist. Over the span of these movements, artists increasingly focused on the intrinsic qualities of their media—e.g., line, form, and colour—and moved away from inherited notions of art." (Kuiper)

Modern Art: Abstract art, Cubism, Pop art, Minimalism, Dadaism

Artists: Picasso, Braque, Matisse, Kandinsky, Mondrian

Music: Stravinsky, George Antheil, Schoenberg, See: "The Rite of Spring" by Stravinsky as a landmark work

Dance: "The Rite of Spring" Ballet, "Les Noces" Ballet, Isadora Duncan, Loie Fuller, Ruth St. Denis

Literature: "Ulysses" James Joyce, "Metamorphosis" and "The Trail" Franz Kafka, "The Waste Land" T.S. Elliot, "Crime and Punishment"

Fyodor Dostoyevsky, "Diabolidad" and "The Master and Margarita" Mikhail Bulgakov

Architecture: Frank Lloyd Wright, Le Corbusier, Walter Gropius, Mies van der Rohe

(Source: "Modernism", 2020)

Modern ideas: Faith in science, Development and progress, Democracy, The individual, A meritocratic social order, Humanity can recreate nature by virtue of her reason (Freinacht, "2017")

Post-Modernism

"Postmodernism is a broad movement that developed in the mid- to late 20th century across philosophy, the arts, architecture, and criticism, marking a departure from modernism. The term has been more generally applied to describe a historical era said to follow after modernity and the tendencies of this era ... Postmodernism is generally defined by an attitude of skepticism, irony, or rejection toward what it describes as the grand narratives and ideologies associated with modernism, often criticizing Enlightenment rationality and focusing on the role of ideology in maintaining political or economic

power. Postmodern thinkers frequently describe knowledge claims and value systems as contingent or socially-conditioned, describing them as products of political, historical, or cultural discourses and hierarchies. Common targets of postmodern criticism include universalist ideas of objective reality, morality, truth, human nature, reason, science, language, and social progress. Accordingly, postmodern thought is broadly characterized by tendencies to self-consciousness, self-referentiality, epistemological and moral relativism, pluralism, and irreverence."

("Postmodernism", 2020)

Like any rebuttal within history, whether political, religious, or economical, we find that the rebuttal to modernism emerges post-modernism. The idea that the sincere building for a greater society, lifting up through the lens of the "dignity of man" and the emergence of the industrial revolution to provide meaning and purpose held flaws. The post-modernist emerged as a rebuttal to point out the flaws and voice the opinion in opposition to the path in which modernism was headed through an angst-driven ironic form of narrative. A disruption to the modernist society in which the hope of the post-modernist is to have those rooted deeply within modernism to stop and observe the world in which they live and contribute. Post-modernism is a method of dialogue in which to create observations about the current state of the modern world.

This movement emerged during the mid 21st century and has become the mainstream narrative of culture. The discourse of modern day 2020 revolves around political, historical, cultural and hierarchical narratives that exist in extremism. From the COVID-19 pandemic, the current political climate in Washington DC, the protests, riots, crime and continuing narrative of topics such as gender, race, equality, and extreme political allegiance through media, entertainment, news and social media has fueled a skeptical grand narrative against ideologies associated with modernism. Tearing down old systems, destroying monuments, protesting main street (when the problem is politicians and corporations). The postmodern narrative is fueling entertainment and media as a cultural discourse to redefine and criticize morality, truth, human nature, reason, science and social progress. As if to say, the old systems are broken and we must destroy it all and rebuild in the manner in which the postmodernist deems to be correct. However, the earlier quote states that postmodernism "often criticizes(ing)...on the role of ideology in maintaining political or economic power." And this narrative is running its course across culture.

Post-modernism is positive, when applied to the minority way of thinking within a large system. In which the skeptic reflects, evaluates and critically determines the inequities and imbalances of a system. For the individual, postmodernism can help on a journey of personal growth, self-reflection, self awareness and self consciousness. The irreverence of postmodernism exemplified on a larger mainstream cultural platform only leads to a path of destruction. History reveals this time and again.

"In the late 20th century a reaction against Modernism set in. Architecture saw a return to traditional materials and forms and sometimes to the use of decoration for the sake of decoration itself, as in the work of Michael Graves and, after the 1970s, that of Philip Johnson. In literature, irony and self-awareness became the postmodern fashion and the blurring of fiction and nonfiction a favoured method. Such writers as Kurt Vonnegut, Thomas Pynchon, and Angela Carter employed a postmodern approach in their work." (Kuiper)

Postmodernism can be a healthy reaction to modernism. In which the cultural creators of our time can step back, observe and create new works in a way which pokes and prods at the current modernist system. The narrative becomes a problem when it exceeds the postmodernist's intent and becomes the grand narrative of a society in which isn't ready or capable of understanding the depth of postmodernism.

Duignan goes on to suggest that postmodernism is a denial of general philosophical viewpoints. To this, it becomes clear that postmodernism was the skeptical lens in which some viewed the impact and effects the modernist movement had on society.

"Postmodernism is largely a reaction against the intellectual assumptions and values of the modern period in the history of Western philosophy (roughly, the 17th through the 19th century). Indeed, many of the doctrines characteristically associated with postmodernism can fairly be described as the straightforward denial of general philosophical viewpoints that were taken for granted during the 18th-century Enlightenment, though they were not unique to that period. " (Duignan)

There is debate about where we are in the movement of postmodernism today. Some would say it has ended, others say we are experiencing a post-postmodern world, and others would say that we are in transition to something else yet to be defined. The blending and transition from postmodernism to wherever we are headed in the future is widely debated. I am under the thought that in order for us to move forward, we need to accept that the current conditions of culture, especially mainstream progressive thought, is evidence of postmodernism. And for us to move beyond, we must accept that the break from postmodernism is essential to this path forward. Some would argue that we are currently existing within a modern world, striving for more postmodern ideals. I disagree. We are witnessing evidence in realtime across the globe of postmodernism being implemented in social, political, economical and cultural dynamics by those in power who were raised and grew up during the height of disruption and a lens for change under the narrative of postmodernism. That is to say, they are influenced and informed to create progressive change today from the postmodern ideals that have informed their past upbringings.

"We do not wish to suggest that all postmodern tendencies are over and done with. But we do believe many of them are taking another shape, and, more importantly, a new sens, a new meaning and direction. For one, financial crises, geopoli- tical instabilities, and climatological uncertainties have necessitated a reform of the economic system ("un nouveau monde, un nouveau capitalisme", but also the transition from a white collar to a green collar economy). For another, the disintegration of the political center on both a geo- political level (as a result of the rise to prominence of the Eastern economies) and a national level (due to the failure of the "third way", the polarization of localities, ethnicities, classes, and the influence of the Internet blogosphere) has required a restructuration of the political discourse. Similarly, the need for a decentralized produc- tion of alternative energy; a solution to the waste of time, space, and energy caused by (sub)urban sprawls; and a sustainable urban future have demanded a transformation of our material landscape. Most significantly perhaps, the cultural industry has responded in kind,

increasingly abandoning tactics such as pastiche and parataxis for strategies like myth and metaxis, melancholy for hope, and exhibitionism for engagement. We will return to these strategies in more detail shortly." (Timotheus Vermeulen & Robin van den Akker (2010) Notes on metamodernism, Journal of Aesthetics & Culture)

This idealism exists as a way to hold onto the values of the past, while looking forward to the future. Human nature has created constructs in society where we derive a set of beliefs and values to carry us into the future. In the past, that future transformed itself into the modernist structure of society in which the collective built roads, bridges, monuments, architecture, ideas, printing presses, automobiles, communication, newspapers, and the modern instruments of the world that drive our lives, economics and livelihoods forward. In such a way, we now look at the past, which was once the present and an idea of the future through the lens of the postmodernist where we see the flaws. We see the cracks in the system. We see the failures of how modernism may have left some behind as we continue to press on toward the future. Those cracks become amplified and serve as a narrative for postmodernism to derive their fuel through art, culture, media and entertainment. What was once the vision of a postmodernist to create a world in which the skepticism of their perceptions would be addressed, we now see these ideals as being the mainstream topics of cultural movements of today. Where the cracks are one side of the culture, and the drive forward through modernist progress and ideals are the alternative. And the polarities become more extreme between the two.

So we look back through history. The access to information, knowledge and ideas create a space in which we become nostalgic for simpler times. We desire to have the values of yesterday in which were created by those who desired a better future. And we look at where culture has emerged from and we are unhappy with the results, moreso within ourselves and then we project those personal inadequacies as a grander narrative in which everything must be wrong if I might be wrong. And the continual wheel of these narratives progress.

Skepticism is healthy when rooted in mitigating risk or trying to find a better solution. To exist as the skeptic simply for the sake of being the skeptic provides zero value to the individual or to society as a whole. In which, the skeptic must also realize that the apathy in which follows skepticism is not because of lack of success, or lack of effort, or failure. But the apathy now becomes the result of the narrative instead of pursuing a better solution. The skeptic gets caught in giving up hope because they either do not have a solution, or they give up when their initial idea or solution isn't as great as they intended. Combine this with the "snowflake" "everyone gets a trophy" "helicopter parenting" culture and it creates a cocktail of self-entitlement. The postmodern skeptic becomes apathetic because their solution isn't valid. Or they fail to continue the pursuit of finding a valid solution. The narrative then shifts from skeptic to apathy in which apathy breeds a lazy form of "maintaining political or economic power" rooted in the postmodern narratives driving mainstream media.

My hope is that our future will go beyond this narrative. Beyond the apathy, beyond the lazy thinking, beyond the cultural battle for "who's right and who's wrong". Where skepticism can be healthy and then the solutions in which may have bred apathy for the postmodernist is course corrected to continue focusing on finding solutions. However, this problem solving approach is not widely understood or known or explored. Our education system, ran by postmodernists, prime children to learn, memorize and pass tests. The real world requires critical thinking and the ability to continue a pursuit in the face of failure. There is no guarantee. We are conditioned to believe that our first idea is the correct idea and anything outside of the confines of traditional education is merely left to chance and imagination and being "brilliant" or "creative". I'm here to tell you, creativity is not a gift, or magic or a talent or for the incredibly intelligent. Creativity is a process in which you cease to give up after your first round of revisions and feedback is less than you anticipated. Creativity is not a single stroke of brilliance in which you are entitled to. Creativity is not a word you throw on your resume, or study in school. Creativity is the lifelong pursuit of exploring beyond the failures. In which multiple failures lead you to the path of discovering the best solution after having sifted through all the failures to get you there. Postmodernism falls apart after the skeptic doesn't get their way the first time. Creativity falls apart when it becomes overrun with postmodern thinking when the requirement for creativity involves a longlasting pursuit and fortitude to continue discovering beyond the failures. Postmodernism gives "creatives" a gold star and a trophy for showing up and then blame the lack of impact and ROI for a project on the culture.

> *"We would like to make it absolutely clear that this new shape, meaning, and direction do not directly stem from some kind of post-9/11 sentiment. Terrorism neither infused doubt about the supposed superiority of neoliberalism, nor did it inspire reflection about the basic assumptions of Western economics, politics, and culture*quite the contrary. The conservative reflex of the "war on terror" might even be taken to symbolize a reaffirmation of postmodern values.16 The threefold "threat" of the credit crunch, a collapsed center, and climate change has the opposite effect, as it infuses doubt, inspires reflection, and incites a move forward out of the postmodern and into the metamodern." (Timotheus*

Vermeulen & Robin van den Akker (2010) Notes on metamodernism,
Journal of Aesthetics & Culture)

Postmodernism exists as the status quo within culture. Those who have hinged their beliefs upon the postmodernist worldview are now the gatekeepers, creators, leaders of society in which they once sought to disrupt and change. They are now in the drivers seats of companies, brands, movements and politics in which they are using the system to redefine from within the system. The translation to this is the growing emergence of typical trends, aesthetics, ideas and narratives that were prevalent during the postmodernists movements of the 1980s and 1990s, but they now exist at the forefront of our cultural mainstream. Stories, topics, aesthetics, fashion, political ideology, all exist as a form of post-modernism that was once seen as radical or disruptive - hiding away in the corners of society in which you had to seek a subculture in order to find these ideals.

Everything in which was seen as strange, weird, queer, "out there", oddball, underground during my adolescent is now the formative ideas and aesthetics creating mainstream culture. In which, those very things were so obscure during the prime era of postmodernism, it is now the backdrop for our cultural landscape in film, music, art, politics and religion.

And, as history shows us, postmodern ideology at such a large influence, has damaging and terrible repercussions.

Evidence of Post-Modernism - "Irony"

Emerging from modernism comes postmodernism within society and the Western world. Much like political or religious ideas, post-modernism was a rebuttal to the ideals embraced within modernism. This rebuttal began to question the very systems, ideals and progress that had been built, achieved and continued within the constructs of society. The ideals informed culture, art, commerce and industry. From this, emerged a new philosophy to go against and question these modernist ideas through irreverence, disruption and irony.

"Postmodernism is generally defined by an attitude of skepticism, irony, or rejection of the grand narratives and ideologies of modernism, often calling into question various assumptions of Enlightenment rationality. Consequently, common targets of postmodern critique include universalistnotions of objective reality, morality, truth, human nature, reason, science, language, and social progress. Postmodern thinkers frequently call attention to the contingent or socially-conditioned nature of knowledgeclaims and value systems, situating them as products of particular political, historical, or cultural discourses and hierarchies. Accordingly, postmodern thought is broadly characterized by tendencies to self-referentiality, epistemological and moral relativism, pluralism, and irreverence." ("Postmodernism", 2020)

Architecture ("Postmodernism", 2020):

The Language of Post-Modern Architecture, first published in 1977, and since running to seven editions. Charles Jencks makes the point that Post-Modernism (like Modernism) varies for each field of art, and that for architecture it is not just a reaction to Modernism but what he terms double coding: "Double Coding: the combination of Modern techniques with something else (usually traditional building) in order for architecture to communicate with the public and a concerned minority, usually other architects." ("Postmodernism", 2020)

Art: "Postmodern art is a body of art movements that sought to contradict some aspects of modernism or some aspects that emerged or developed in its aftermath. Cultural production manifesting as intermedia, installation art, conceptual art, deconstructionist display, and multimedia, particularly involving video, are described as post-modern."

Graphic Design: "Early mention of postmodernism as an element of graphic design appeared in the British magazine, "Design." A char-acteristic of postmodern graphic design is that "retro, techno, punk, grunge, beach, parody, and pastiche were all conspicuous trends. Each had its own sites and venues, detractors and advocates."

Literature: "Pierre Menard, Author of the Quixote" Jorge Luis Borg-es'. Samuel Beckett, Vladimir Nabokov, William Gaddis, Umberto Eco, Pier Vittorio Tondelli, John Hawkes, William S. Burroughs, Giannina Braschi, Kurt Vonnegut, John Barth, Jean Rhys, Donald Barthelme, E.L. Doctorow, Richard Kalich, Jerzy Kosiñski, Don DeLillo, Thomas, Pynchon, Ishmael Reed, Kathy Acker, Ana Lydia Vega, Jåchym Topol, Paul Auster

Music: Terry Riley, Henryk Górecki, Bradley Joseph, John Adams,

Steve Reich, Philip Glass, Michael Nyman, Lou Harrison, John Cage, Art Rock genre, Talking Heads, Laurie Anderson, The Pet Shop Boys, "Ladies and Gentleman We Are Floating in Space" Spiritualized, "Disco Volante" Mr. Bungle, "My Beautiful Dark Twisted Fantasy" Kanye West

Current artists who embrace post-modernism within their work in "pop culture": Billie Ellish, Kanye West, Sturgil Simpson

Television ("Postmodernism", 2020) (IMDB, 2020): Portlandia, Family Guy, Modern Family, Community, South Park, Bob's Burgers, Breaking Bad, Ed Edd & Eddy (Deeley, 2016)

Film: Pulp Fiction, Fight Club, Watchmen, American Gangster, Inherent Vice, 3 From Hell, Paris Texas, Payback, Jawbreaker, Far From Heaven, Titus, Close-Up, Youth Without Youth, American Desert, Being Black Enough, Jealous Gods, Phantom, Diamonds in the Sky, Fragile Machine, The Postmodern Pioneer Plaque, The Next Scorsese, Haemophobia("IMDB", 2020)

Postmodern ideas: Critical questioning of all knowledge and science, Suspicion towards all grand narratives about "progress", Emphasis on symbols and contexts, Ironic distance, Cultures have been oppressed and ruined by modern society, Reveals injustice in "democratic" societies, Relations create the individual, A multicultural order where the weak are included, Humanity has destroyed the biosphere (Source: Freinacht, "2017")

Metamodernism

"Metamodernism is a proposed set of developments in philosophy, aesthetics, and culture which emerge from and react to postmodernism. One definition characterizes metamodernism as mediations between aspects of both modernism and postmodernism ...The prefix "meta-" here referred not to a reflective stance or repeated rumination, but to Plato's metaxy, which denotes a movement between opposite poles as well as beyond them. Vermeulen and van den Akker described metamodernism as a "structure of feeling" that oscillates between modernism and postmodernism like "a pendulum swinging between...innumerable poles". According to Kim Levin, writing in ARTnews, this oscillation "must embrace doubt, as well as hope and melancholy, sincerity and irony, affect and apathy, the personal and the political, and technology and techne." For the metamodern generation, according to Vermeulen, "grand narratives are as necessary as they are problematic, hope is not simply something to distrust, love not necessarily something to be ridiculed." ("Metamodernism", 2020)

And so we witness the simultaneous happenings of both modernism and postmodernism ideals existing at the same time. Within ourselves. Within our society. Within our lives and community. The oscillation between the sincere and ironic are happening all around us. Infused within and without the world we live, the media we consume, the ideas we concern ourselves with and our attempt to make sense of meaning for ourselves, but also our purpose within the greater context of the world. This discussion has been happening for quite sometime. We listen to words and phrases like "rhetoric" or "grand narrative" infused in either a modernist or postmodernist worldview on a topic. We are fed similar notions of these ideas from both sides of (a)political, (a)religious, and cultural narratives occurring in our lives. However, the happenings within various parts of the world are now a direct concern to our daily lives because those happenings are informing our world at both a local and global level. The pendulum swings. The polarity exists. And yet, to make sense of this we are forced to choose one side or the other, choose good over evil, or choose the lesser of two evils.

However, the idea and term of Metamodernism has been around since the 1970s as a predictor and describer of sorts as to what comes after postmodernism. And when postmodernism becomes the status quo, it is no longer effective, instead, it becomes destructive. So we try to describe and observe the next movement in culture and society. And that exists as the idea of "Metamodernism" - where both modernism and postmodernism exist at the same time. However, we do not need to choose one or the other, but they exist as "both/and" and within that - we make sense of our personal lives and discover truth in this ever changing landscape of local and global ideals.

And from this, we exist within the constructs of the current society. Bombarded by influences, media, advertisements and marketing that represent both a sincerity and also an irony to it all. The meaning in the meaningless. There is everything and there is nothing. We have access to information, knowledge, ideas, connections yet we feel more isolated and alone than ever before. The growing numbers of anxiety and depression have continued to rise. It feels as if we are slogging through our own existence, watching the global policies and ideals move us in virtuous, idealistic or hopeful directions - and when those are achieved, we aren't convinced that they will make us any more happy. The polarity of the societal differences surpasses extremes we have ever witnessed, or where privy too. Yet, we can't do much about it. We are aware of the troubles in the world, but the powers that be are assuring us each day that "they've got it handled" but we aren't too sure about that.

This structure of feeling puts us in a place of uncertainty. And they like it that way. (They being those who influence us). We are tossed around like emotional rag dolls trying to make sense between truth and fiction. One side holds truth and the other fiction, until we discover the fiction is everywhere. And the truth may have been lost along the way.

"In short, cultural philosophies help us make sense of our times by seeing patterns in how entire cultures (and individual subcultures within those cultures) operate. And because American culture, like any culture, has political and economic subcultures as well as ones in which new art is regularly being made, metamodernism gives us a lens through which to consider nearly everything that's happened in America since the invention of the internet: political, socioeconomic, and sociocultural." (Abramson, 2017)

My notion is that truth exists between both modern and postmodern ideals. That in order to really get to the heart of society, we must choose to exist between both modernism and postmodernism. To take the truth from each, the fiction from each, to consciously move forward in our own lives without being swayed from one side or the other as both movements and cultural ideologies are fighting for our attention, our loyalty and our allegiance. However, the polarity creates tension within the self, tension within our community and tension within the world. There is positive and negatives to both modernism and postmodernism, and the forward approach to this must not exist within choosing one or the other at the equal scale in which they exist, but to consciously exist between both to discover real truth.

> *"The ecosystem is severely disrupted, the financial system is increasingly uncontrollable, and the geopolitical structure has recently begun to appear as unstable as it has always been uneven. This triple crisis infuses doubt and inspires reflection about our basic assumptions, as much as inflaming cultural debates and provoking dogmatic entrenchments. History, it seems, is moving rapidly beyond its all too hastily proclaimed end." ("Notes on Metamodernsim", 2010)*

The polarity of movements oscillating from both modern and postmodern sensibilities are diverging further and further apart. The best way to describe this sense is to consider the idea of a pendulum. We swing back and forth through our daily lives. The rhetoric in culture and media is becoming more extreme from both ends of this pendulum. We are caught in the middle, yet we are forced, sociologically, to choose a side in order to fit within societal norms. One side or the other. The modernist extreme or the post-modernist extreme. And we also become bombarded with alternative viewpoints in our media consumption, our news, cultural movements and ideas to where the confusion is meant to distort the truth in a way to pander to one side or the other. We must pick a side and say that the other side is the evil, antagonist, villain in our story.

However, at the core of who we are, as humans, we seemingly have lost our way. Our identities are tied to the oscillation of one side or the other. And we feel trapped, but the alternative is to feel confusion and distortion.

I believe that within this continuing polarity of extremes, we must seek to find real truth. And that truth doesn't not exist within a single approach to either modern or postmodernism. As the world is rapidly evolving and changing and progressing to becoming a more technological and interconnected planet, we cannot hinge the ideals and values of either/or (from modernism or post-modernism) in this new era of humanity across the planet. We need to find truth within the polarity extremes.

There are positives and negatives to both modernism and postmodernism.

We should be careful and weary of those who speak of metamodernism from a foundation of postmodernist ideals. Only until we choose to revert back to the ancient truths of humanity, the foundations of western civilization and the principles in which have built the modern world are recognized - then can we combine those ideals with thoughtful critique, questioning, articulation, scientific methods and understanding a new way of process and progress. To ground our foundation forward from the post-modernist foundation is built upon shaky ground that is only meant to exist as a disruptor of the modernist ideals in which post-modernism eventually emerged. Logically it makes zero sense to support metamodernism through a post-modernist viewpoint - and frankly, it reads deceptive.

The postmodernist used technology and media as a tool to disrupt the old world notion of the modernist movement. From this disruption emerges new leaders, businesses, technology, platforms and cultural influence built from those who embraced post-modernism. These platforms now exist as behemoths in society ran by those and supported by communities in which postmodernism is prevalent. Jeff Bezos, Steve Jobs, Elon Musk, Bill Gates - all postmodernists who saw the opportunity to change culture - for the better - through a post-modernist viewpoint. Those pillars of technology have now influenced and informed society through a network culture in which the gatekeepers of the past are no longer relevant to the outcomes of the future. The modernists existed as the gatekeepers of society, in which order, vision, hierarchy and structure built foundations in which the future of progress could be laid. Those gatekeepers are either dismantled, no longer relevant, or shifting their business to become more post-modern.

"Since the turn of the millennium, moreover, the democratization of digital technologies, techniques and tools has caused a shift from a postmodern media logic characterized by television screen and spectacle, cyberspace and simulacrum towards a metamodern media logic of creative amateurs, social networks and locative media – what the cultural theorist Kazys Varnelis calls network culture." ("Notes on Metamodernism", 2010)

The strength of the new narrative is not in the power structure in which communicates, but through the conscious and subconscious network in which we formulate our worldview. We believe that we are contributing to culture and society, which instead, we are merely a product to push the larger narrative of technology and power formulated through a post-modern leadership narrative. We are fooling ourselves otherwise.

For metamodernism to exist, we should agree that both modern and postmodern movements are happening simultaneously. The notion that some who believe metamodernism is emerging because we are still within the modernist movement means that we need to embrace more post-modern ideals is essentially wrong. Those who speak of this notion fundamentally still embrace the ideals of post-modernism in a way in which they now disguise it and shift their narrative to say that the ideals in prominent societies of today that are not working is essentially the flaws and failures of modernism. However, the socialization of Scandinavian countries, the ideals built on empty foundations and the push for total science and empathy without the belief or recognition of modernism and post-modernism occurring simultaneously is essentially post-modern in it's form.

I am hesitant to agree with those who believe that metamodernism is a shift away from only current modernist ideals because the under-current of the argument exists as a way to undermine modernism while doubling down on post-modern values. However, the post-modernist path throughout history has led to destruction in society if not carefully managed. We see these examples time and again, Soviet Russia being one example, a pathway emerged from post-modernism.

The problem is that postmodernists will not admit that postmodernism has failed. Instead, those who speak the loudest about metamodernism tend to do so as a mask to push and support a belief rooted in a post-modern foundation. I fundamentally disagree with these descriptions and narratives about metamodernism. Whereas, metamodernism exists when both modern and post-modern ideals can be recognized as having equal prominence in society - and their positives and negatives can be equally measured. We cannot use metamodernism to dismantle modernism while pushing for more post-modernism. This is a dangerous path that does not end well, as history has shown.

"Our methodological assumption is that the dominant cultural prac-

tices and the dominant aesthetic sensibilities of a certain period form, as it were, a 'discourse' that expresses cultural moods and common ways of doing, making and thinking. To speak of a structure of feeling (or a cultural dominant) therefore has the advantage, as Jameson once explained, that one does not "obliterate difference and project an idea of the historical period as massive homogeneity. [It is] a conception which allows for the presence and coexistence of a range of very different, yet subordinate features." ("Notes on Metamodernism", 2010)

And through the range of combing different, oscillating, subordinate features within our work, reflected and supported through a discourse built from a cultural dominant sensibility, we can then combine the polarities of both modern and post-modern sensibilities into new work that will support a new sense of opportunity, feeling, inspiration and search for meaning - between the polarity extremes in which our local, global and technology globalized society is operating from in the current landscape. From here, we can start to derive new ways of being, creating and communicating into the world where the focus first creates a sense of tension but ultimately allows the audience to experience a new feeling of metamodernism in which they experience and determine those sensibilities for themselves. We then consider how might we create new ideas, platforms, opportunities and ideas in which these ranges of feelings and features can be examined, created, displayed, experienced and highlighted in new and interesting ways where the dialogue shifts from either a heavily focused modernist or post-modern narrative.

From here, truth (and new sensibilities of truth) can be explored, discovered and experienced as we shift from a modernist and postmodernist foundation.

"These different, yet subordinate features can alternatively be de-scribed as 'residuals' of days gone by or as 'emergents' that point to another day and age. Postmodernism might have passed, it might have "given up the ghost", but, as Josh Toth rightly argues, to speak of its death is to also speak of its afterlife. "The death of postmodern-ism (like all deaths) can also be viewed as a passing, a giving over of a certain inheritance, that this death (like all deaths) is also a living on, a passing on." The spectre of postmodernism – but also that of modernism – still haunts contemporary culture." ("Notes on Metamodernism", 2010)

The haunting of both exist as a murky uncertain wave of cultural narratives and movements in which all are battling for some sort fo relevance or significance. As if to fight for the next hierarchical power structure which will emerge beyond modern and postmodernism. The emergence is thought be fought and won through the narratives we are seeing played out through media, entertainment, culture and politics. However, I believe a different kind of world exists in the future, where we can look at both sides of modern and postmodernism and discover that both might exist together through a new sense of being. Where the audience is waking up because the centuries long show and dance has now ended. We can safely exit the building and go on about our business. We can take from it what we want and decide to think for ourselves beyond the narratives in which we are sold and must choose within the constructs of modern day.

"Others have started to theorise emergent structures of feeling that might, or might not, become dominant in the (not so near) future. The

most obvious examples of such an emergence are all those practices that have become associated with the commons. Several theorists have argued, for instance, that these practices, ultimately, point towards an altermodernity, a future beyond modernity as we currently know it. Whether or not we agree with these visions of the future is besides the point here. What matters is that it is our contemporary culture that enables these visions; or rather, that opens up the discourse of having a vision at all." ("Notes on Metamodernism", 2010)

We now exist in a time and space within civilization in which we can think upon these things. We can look back throughout history and learn from the ebb and flows of cultural movements, societies, wars, rise to power, downfall of empires, etc. We exist in a time where we can reflect back and consider the path forward. Those who exist within modern or postmodern ideologies consider the path forward to be through their own bias thinking. In which, their own self interests and ideologies inform the notion that their way is the path to truth because it yields them to be right. No one wants to be wrong. The gatekeepers of society want to keep us following their paths. They want us to continue to follow through the polarity of either modern or postmodern thought in which to say they want to help us. They are looking out for our best interests. However, the path forward might be where we can look at the landscape of civilization, the current condition of culture and the longing desire within human nature. Through this, we might uncover a new path where both modernism and postmodernism emerge to provide some new sensibility of a different kind of future. I have my personal opinions on the matter, however, I don't want to spoil this with those personal thoughts. I want you to find and discover the meaning of your own path beyond modern and postmodernism and uncover real truth beyond what others tell you.

> *"If, epistemologically, the modern and the post- modern are linked to Hegel's "positive" idealism, the metamodern aligns itself with Kant's "negative" idealism. Kant's philosophy of history after all, can also be most appropriately summarized as "as-if" thinking. As Curtis Peters explains, according to Kant, "we may view human history as if mankind had a life narrative which describes its self-movement toward its full rational/social potential . . . to view history as if it were the story of mankind's development". Indeed, Kant himself adopts the as-if terminology when he writes "[e]ach . . . people, as if following some guiding thread, go toward a natural but to each of them unknown goal".19 That is to say, humankind, a people, are not really going toward a natural but unknown goal, but they pretend they do so that they progress morally as well as politically. Metamodernism moves for the sake of moving, attempts in spite of its inevitable failure; it seeks forever for a truth that it never expects to find. If you will forgive us for the banality of the metaphor for a moment, the metamodern thus willfully adopts a kind of donkey-and-carrot double-bind. Like a donkey it chases a carrot that it never manages to eat because the carrot is always just beyond its reach. But precisely because it never manages to eat the carrot, it never ends its chase, setting foot in moral realms the modern donkey (having eaten its carrot elsewhere) will never encounter, entering political domains*

the postmodern donkey (having aban- doned the chase) will never come across". (Timotheus Vermeulen & Robin van den Akker (2010) Notes on metamodernism, Journal of Aesthetics & Culture)

In this regard, if evidence of metamodernism proves that the movement of culture and society is in fact moving within the direction of hurling forward through life where the truth in which we seek always seems to exist just out of reach, then how can we approach the work of design in an effort to compliment or acknowledge this sentiment? What role does design play in a world where we exist to move forward without ever finding what we are looking for. Beyond the discipline of design, we as a designer, must be aware that our own worldview, biases, politics, religions, and beliefs have effected and impacted our work. From the modernist designer to the post-modern designer.

The things we design end up designing us. As much as we wish to think we are creating the future, we have become merely the reflections of our past. We are designing within silos and echoes chambers, unbeknownst to ourselves that we are simply designing in a race to the bottom. Design has commodified itself. The tools we have built, the internet we helped create, the ideas in which we share have become the same artifacts that seek to make us replaceable. However, I believe in a deeper calling and meaning for design. One in which causes us to uncomfortably step aside from our own single mined perception of the world, and seek to view the world from a different angle. Where the validity and invalidity of both modern and post-modern ideals help to form a designer's perspective about the current world in an effort to recognize, observe and determine how in which we move forward. And that movement exists in a place in which we must also decide to step aside and allow our work to help others see and experience the polarity for themselves. In which they begin to make sense of the world, the movements, their own existence and a sincere and ironic pursuit of truth amidst the global landscape of modern humanity. We must choose to observe the world around us while consciously considering the future of humanity through a lens of design.

"Ontologically, metamodernism oscillates between the modern and the postmodern. It oscillates between a modern enthusiasm and a postmodern irony, between hope and melancholy, between naïvete and knowingness, empathy and apathy, unity and plurality, totality and fragmentation, purity and ambiguity. Indeed, by oscillating to and fro or back and forth, the metamodern negotiates between the modern and the postmodern. One should be careful not to think of this oscillation as a balance however; rather, it is a pendulum swinging between 2, 3, 5, 10, innumerable poles. Each time the metamodern enthusiasm swings toward fanaticism, gravity pulls it back toward irony; the moment its irony sways toward apathy, gravity pulls it back toward enthusiasm." (Timotheus Vermeulen & Robin van den Akker (2010) Notes on metamodernism, Journal of Aesthetics & Culture)

This sensibility has become magnified through the growth of technology, media, narratives and the changing of our everyday lives. We become a local citizen with a global mindset. Swinging and oscillating back and forth to the ever micro moment of you reading this very sentence to thinking about the global pandemics and economic problems throughout the globe. The mind moves beyond the micro and macro and our sensibility, in order for our sanity, is to pick a path of narratives that help us come to grips with this changing world.

Within this though, I believe that the designer of the future must be aware of these movements and consider of different place within society beyond the modern or postmodern ideological narratives. In which, the designer can be self aware enough to remove themselves from the cultural trappings of these grand narratives and to sit back and observe in which the ability to look at solutions for the future exist in understanding the truth of human nature beyond the cultural narratives. To look beyond the topics of conversation and dive below the surface of these movements. The future will be shaped, not through a polarity winning the argument, but through the new emergence of truth and sensibilities rising to the surface. The alternative is a dystopian future straight out of Orwell's 1984 or Huxely's Brave New World.

And if the evidence of society reveals itself to be both modern and postmodernism simultaneously, the pendulum in which we swing not only has shown itself to move back and forth between modernism and post-modernism, but the movement becomes more rapid and extreme. From political protests, news cycles, the rapid advancements of technology, economic rise and fall, the exponential increase of artificial intelligence, the cultural shifts of equality, equity and balance in workplaces; we are witnessing the pendulum in realtime. We observe the oscillating narra-tives in media, news, entertainment, digital platforms, podcasts and social media. The message is clear and when you observe the world through this lens, you begin to see the undercurrent of truth and deception emerge from all forms of the pendulum.

"It is a worldview which combines the modern faith in progress with the postmodern critique. What you get then, is a view of reality in which people are on a long, complex developmental journey towards greater complexity and existential depth. The metamodern philosophy is a whole world of ideas and suppositions that are counter-intuitive to

modern and postmodern people alike. But since both the modern and postmodern philosophies are increasingly outdated, these metamodern ideas are set to develop, take hold, and spread. One day, they may become as dominant as the modern philosophy is today." (Freinacht)

My hope is that the observation of these drastic shifts in culture can be given a name, metamodernism, and to be recognized within the design industry as a path forward. Not only a path for observing where culture is heading, but a path for design to observe the next evolution and iteration within design. As much as we see the shifts from Classical Design, Computational Design, and Design Thinking - my observations of culture has led me to write the second half of this book, in which serves as a call to designers in a way in which we might observe these grand narratives within our cultures, and unhinge ourselves from our own biases to become self-aware in which the role a designer exists in the future sits between both modernism and postmodernism. For sake of the this writing, I will attach the term "metamodernism" moving forward in order to describe this sensibility in which design might operate from.

I envision a new path for design to think beyond the execution of the work. In which our work in design first begins with ourselves and that work becomes the starting point in which the future impact of our work emerges. Beyond the work, we must become conscious and self-aware of our own existence within the oscillating pendulum of Metamodernism, and find a new way to observe both/and in order to build a better future. The second part of this book aims to address these initial ideas and opportunities as a Designer.

I deeply wish that design will encourage us to consider the depths of our own humanity first. In which we go beyond the narratives within culture and seek to truly understand and empathize beyond the current talking points and topics of today. To understand humanity and the human level beyond the intersections of identities.

Overall, I hope for design to help us shape a new path beyond the polarity of the pendulum. Between modern and postmodern happening in extreme throughout culture. I hope designers will step beyond these polarities and choose a new path - starting with the self, observing and self awareness, and translating the truth uncovered between both/and of modern and postmodern ideologies to create a future grounded in truth.

Evidence of Metamodernism

Today we exist within a world where evidence of both modernism and post-modernism exist. They inform our lives at various touch points and work as polar opposites within the confines of our lives, culture, news, media and entertainment. The existence of both has created greater extremes related to economics, politics, religion, culture and information. We are caught within both trying to make sense of this new grand narrative at an individual and global scale to understand new meanings related to our own lives and our purpose in a greater globally connected world.

Metamodernism is a termed used to describe a set of ethics and ideology of a world that exists beyond post-modernism. It is the existence of both modernism and post-modernism simultaneously happening. Some have also referred to this as post-postmodernism.

It is the marriage of two worlds: modern and postmodern ideals. Existing as the progress of perspective, metamodernism captures the emotional connection and feeling between mind, body and spirit - but addresses the tension and uncertainty within. Ideas around our soul, humanity and emotional development lean into a feeling that both modernism and postmodernism have yet to fulfill. Culture has explored both at mainstream levels and yet we still have a yearning sense of sadness, loneliness, disconnect from each other. So we ask "what next?". If modernism or post-modernism are not the answer. Could metamodernism offer new ideas and ways of thinking that capture the human essence we have long searched for between the drastic pendulum swing of modern to post-modern ideals? Between both lies some form of truth. Being suspended emotionally between both prompts an internal examination of the self at both an individual and global role of our own existence.

Metamodernism takes a less judgmental position between modern-ism and post-modernism. Where both modern and post-modern ideals are pointing fingers at each other, metamodernism considers a world in which values from both can exist at the same time - and within those values, the individual is left to explore and understand the feelings and sentiment of the self between both.

This requires the development of subtle thinking. Looking within to understand and explore the suspended space of feeling that may often bring tension of uncomfortable uncertainty. It requires the individual to develop a stronger sense of self and stronger sense of internal identifi-cation to not be swayed or thrown about amidst the storms of modern or post-modern ideas and narratives. This path becomes the core to the metamodernist.

Examples of metamodernism being introduced exist in the form of meditation in schools, support structures and the relevance of faith dur-ing pandemics or uncertainty within a global society.

The political landscape is filled with evidence of metamodernism. Not for the politicians or the policies or parties. But for the constituents who are given varying narratives and half truths born out of a desire to build party loyalty at the expense of giving up our power and allegiance to red team or blue team.

"Every country has a political culture — widely shared beliefs, values, and norms that define the relationship between citizens and

government, and citizens to one another. Beliefs about economic life are part of the political culture because politics affects economics. A good understanding of a country's political culture can help make sense of the way a country's government is designed, as well as the political decisions its leaders make." (USHistory.org, "2019")

The political divide in America has become prominent since the 1990s. The political landscape has been divided through politicians, mainstream media, 24-hour news cycles and pushing policy based on narratives for over two decades.

"By 2017, the divide had significantly shifted towards the two extremes of the consistently liberal/conservative scale. Median Democrat and Republican sentiment also moved further apart, especially for politically engaged Americans." (Ghosh, "2017")

Pew Research has tracked the political divide in the United States based on surveys of over 5,000 adults. Tracking public sentiment and political polarization since 1994.

Economy

"Between 60–70% of Democrats and Republicans agree that U.S. involvement in the global economy is positive, because it provides the country with access to new markets. However, they diverge when asked about the fairness of the economic system itself. 50% of Republicans think it is fair to most Americans, but 82% of Democrats think it un-

fairly favors powerful interests."(Ghosh, "2017")

Environment

"When it comes to climate change, both Democrats and Republicans see that there is growing evidence for global warming, but they are not sold on the reasons why. 78% of Democrats see human activity as the cause, while only 24% of Republicans agree." (Ghosh, "2017")

Government

"Americans are highly concerned about the U.S. presence on the global stage. Over half (56%) of Democrats think the U.S. should be active in world affairs, while 54% of Republicans think such attention should be focused inward instead of overseas." (Ghosh, "2017")

Society

"There's still a wide partisan divide between Democrats and Republicans on their ideas of government aid (51 p.p. gap), racial equality (45 p.p. gap), immigration (42 p.p. gap), and homosexuality (29 p.p. gap)." (Ghosh, "2017")

Individuals

"Not only this, but partisan animosity is on the rise—81% of Republicans and Democrats find those belonging to the other party equally unfavorable. In fact, both parties have seen a 28 p.p. increase in 'very unfavorable' views of people in the other party, compared to 1994." (Ghosh, "2017")

(For an in-depth review of research related to political polarization, visit https://www.pewresearch.org/topics/political-polarization/)

The political landscape in the United States creates a trickle effect within politics, religions, economics and culture where this divide exists in a growing polarity of extremes that is impacting local communities, state governments and the entire country in relation to the rest of the world as we progress more towards globalization and a global economy.

"It's no longer just Republican vs. Democrat, or liberal vs. conservative. It's the 1 percent vs. the 99 percent, rural vs. urban, white men against the world. Climate doubters clash with believers. Bathrooms have become battlefields, borders are battle lines. Sex and race, faith and ethnicity ... the melting pot seems to be boiling over." (Associated Press, "2020")

Initially coined "The term metamodernist appeared as early as 1975, when Mas'ud Zavarzadeh isolatedly used it to describe a cluster of aesthetics or attitudes which had been emerging in American literary narratives since the mid-1950s." ("Metamodernism", 2020)

Nothing is everything. Everything is nothing.

Metamodernism has emerged out of the complicated constructs of society. We have built hierarchies and civilizations for the betterment of man to create the current world which has allowed us to evaluate, dismantle, observe and critique our current existence and roles within the world. The idea of metamodernism is a result of the intentional and unintentional design of culture and humanity throughout human history. And so we step into a future of confusion and uncertainty defined by the polarizing truths we seek to understand about ourself and our role within the world.

Metamodernsim exists as the polarizing uncertainty we feel from the current constructs of the modern world. And we must somehow grapple this understanding and make sense of it for our future. Metamodernism was unintentionally designed from the ripple effect of humanity building hierarchies and constructs upon itself to bring us to current day.

The idea of this term relates to an internal feeling within individuals because of the oscillation between sincerity and irony.

"Metamodernism, as we see it, is neither a residual nor an emergent structure of feeling, but the dominant cultural logic of contemporary modernity. As we hope to show in this webzine, the metamodern structure of feeling can be grasped as a generational attempt to surpass postmodernism and a general response to our present, crisis-ridden moment. Any one structure of feeling is expressed by a wide variety of cultural practices and a whole range of aesthetic sensibilities.

These practices and sensibilities are shaped by (and are shaping) so-cial circumstances, as much as they are formed in reaction to previous generations and in anticipation of possible futures. We contend that the contemporary structure of feeling evokes a continuous oscilla-tion between (i.e. meta-) seemingly modern strategies and ostensibly postmodern tactics, as well as a series of practices and sensibilities ultimately beyond (i.e. meta-) these worn out categories." ("Notes on Metamodernism", 2010)

We must choose to understand the nuance along with the global impli-cations of this new feeling and work within the framework of current day to create deeper meaning. However much we view this current state as a problem or challenge, the designer perspective should choose see this as an opportunity to deeply connect to the human condition on a global scale. With understanding and alignment of our intentions, we can create a more meaningful world though the lens of metamodernism.

"In 1995, Canadian literary theorist Linda Hutcheon stated that a new label for what was coming after postmodernism was necessary." ("Metamodernism", 2020)

As cultural trends and history moves progresses, we recognize patterns by looking backwards within society. What once was on the fringe, the underground, the sub culture, becomes the status quo until it dissipates into the next version of itself. In postmodernism we have seen this happen with the 1960's hippie movement, the disco era of the 1970's, the cocaine induced 1980's and the grunge of the 1990's.

For the past 20 years, the internet has allowed short lived nostalgia to relive itself in various factions. This has now emerged as postmodern ideals existing as the status quo. From film, television, music, fashion and art - anyone who has paid attention to the past 50 years of original work within postmodernism can see the remixed attempt of work that exists within pop culture.

Postmodernism is the status quo.

The effects are evident. The style popular of today is a remix of postmodern sub cultures from decades ago. The film approach, topics and stories are reimagined versions of indie films from the early 2000's. The art is a digital remix of nostalgic induced work that calls for the remembrance of a time when print and ink ruled our storefronts. Music is a rehash of bands and artists who sat on the edge of the music industry never getting their big break, but now we see major artists remixing and capitalizing their time, style and angst from underground and unknown artists from yesteryear. The evidence of postmodernism influencing mainstream culture is everywhere.

The 1960s brought on a new set of values, ideals and emerging of postmodernism as evidenced through art, culture, music and industry. Broad examples can point to Andy Warhol for his disruption and com- mentary on commercialism, Jackson Pollock for creating the rise of the art market through abstract work, Woodstock music festival for advocat- ing freedom and liberation.

Steve Jobs, Bill Gates, Jeff Bezos, Elon Musk, Reed Hastings, Ted Sarandos, Steve Wozniak, and Larry Page all built their companies through a lens of growing up and embracing postmodern ideologies. Through the 1960's hippie movements, the use a psychedelic drugs, eastern philosophy, and a desire to be a rebel within their respective industries. These men built new ways to innovate and create beyond the institutions they were competing against. Many people doubted them or didn't see their vision, but they pursued through a belief formed by a postmodern ideology. And this mindset has rippled throughout Silicon Valley, forming a culture of those who aspire to be the next Jobs, Gates or Sarandos. Experimenting in ideologies, micro-dosing mushrooms and psychedelics, communal retreats, and exploring various ideas that shaped and formed the worldview of these leaders.

MTV killed the radio star. And when it hit the airwaves, it completely disrupted an industry while simulatanesouly having an incredible impact on culture. The introduction of visual postmodernism was brought into households 24-hours a day.

The Beetles influenced and changed the landscape of culture at the beginning of the postmodern era.

Elvis changed the face of culture, music and rock n roll during a time when sexuality, masculinity, and self-expression where taboo.

Bob Dylan pushed his story driven music with political undertones giving way to the post-modernist movements.

Kurt Cobain became the poster-child for 90's grunge. A movement pushing postmodernism into the mainstream in the mid 1990's with a flurry of bands and artists from Sup Pop Records, Seattle WA. The hair metal hype was over and a new breed of apathetic angst driven music emerged a new genre that became a mainstream success.

Nirvana, Pearl Jam, Soundgarden, Mudhoney, Temple of the Dog emerged from this genre. In addition, we see the rise of shoegaze bands such as My Bloody Valentine, Ride, Failure, Smashing Pumpkins, Slowdive, Swervedriver, Jesus and the Mary Chain, Staryflyer 59, Radiohead, The Verve, Lush all emerge as a cultural narrative against the modernist movements.

Notable metamodern works and artists from the past decade 2010-

2020: Shia Lebouf, Wes Anderson, @Madebyjimbob, Honey Boy, Fleabag (Television), Postmodern musical influences as mainstream, Post Malone, Billie Ellish, Kanye West's "Jesus is King" album, Childish Gambino, and writings of David Foster Wallace.

Cultural moments that build metamodern sensibility: Occupy Wall Street, Black lives matter, Tea Party Movement, Antifa, COVID-19 U.S. Protests, Alt-right protests, Black Lives Matter Protests, Hong Kong Protests, COVID-19 Pandemic and lockdowns, CHAZ (Seattle, WA), Trump administration press briefings, Covid quarantine and lockdown,, Essential business "marijuana stores open", Essential business "closing church"

Technological tools informing metamodern sensibility: Contact tracing, Artificial Intelligence, Biometrics, Economics, Digital currency, Bitcoin and cryptocurrency, Digital workplace, Video conference calls and meetings.

Metamodern ideas (Freinacht, 2017):

• *How can we reap the best parts of the other two?*

• *Can we create better processes for personal development?*

• *Can we recreate the processes by which society is governed, locally and globally?*

• *Can the inner dimensions of life gain a more central role in society?*

• *How can modern, postmodern and premodern people live together productively?*

• *How can politics be adjusted to an increasingly complex world?*

• *What is the unique role of humanity in the ecosystems of nature?*

(Source: Freinacht, "2017")

The intention behind the work creates a sense of tension and unexplored feeling with the audience. Metamodernism exists as a way to define a feeling. A place between modernism and postmodernism. Where both exist at the same time. What once was a sense of "Either / Or". We exist in a place in time that no matter what side of history you decide to exist, there is a bombardment of messaging, narrative, ideas and discussions coming at you from the other viewpoint.

So we swim through these thoughts and feelings.

Grasping onto the postmodernist view or abhorrently defying it.

And vice versa.

The feeling exists as internal unsettling emotions. We are not sure what to do with this, yet we can't escape. We live within a world where modernism exists as the structures, institutions and frameworks of our world, but we also seek to disrupt, adopt or engage in new forms of ideas or platforms for the convenience of a better life. This unsettling feeling manifests it-self across political, economic, religious, cultural and global paradigms.

As those who doubted the value of the internet now use their iPhones on a daily basis. As those who stayed away from buying items online now rely on Amazon for getting their consumer goods. As those who protested the abominations of uncensored music, are now subjected to dialogue and topics far more crass in a single television show. We exist in a world where both modernism has created the structure and frameworks of society and we are using these structures to build upon it cultural ideals of disruption.

"In 2002, Andre Furlani, analyzing the literary works of Guy Dav-enport, defined metamodernism as an aesthetic that is "afteryet by means of modernism.... a departure as well as a perpetuation. The relationship between metamodernism and modernism was seen as going "far beyond homage, toward a reengagement with modernist method in order to address subject matter well outside the range or interest of the modernists themselves." ("Metamodernism", 2020)

And so the pendulum continues to swing back and forth in culture. And we make an individual decision to choose a side, a narrative, a feel-ing between two choices. One rooted in the modernist way of thinking or the other rooted in the revolutionist postmodern way. And we create tribes and communities through these choices. We join together and adopt of hive-mind for hope of belonging and for fear of being ostracized. And these tribes continue to exist at greater polarities from each other. The extreme right, the extreme left. The traditional institutions or the desire for a new type of product or service. Back and forth.

"In 2007, Alexandra Dumitrescu described metamodernism as partly a
concurrence with, partly an emergence from, and partly a reaction to,
postmodernism, "champion[ing] the idea that only in their interconnec-
tion and continuous revision lie the possibility of grasping the nature of
contemporary cultural and literary phenomena." ("Metamodernism",
2020)

But somewhere between the oscillation of these polar opposites, exists
the idea of "both-and" - not "either/or". You must suspend your initial
thoughts and bias for a moment beyond what you currently believe about
the world through religion, politics, economic, culture and society. Beyond
your moral view of right and wrong (or even if you don't believe in right
and wrong - this is still a choice) - or even if you don't believe that we have
a choice but exist within a determinist world. Suspend these ideas you have
about yourself and world. Sit within the space between your own beliefs
and the beliefs of those who have the polar opposite beyond your own
individual views of the world. Beyond right and wrong. Your beliefs may
exist at one end of the polarity formed by the external influence, ideology,
environmental, cultural and political...well, brainwashing... that you are
subjected to - whether you are aware of it or it. Think beyond that for a moment. And evaluate where the pendulum of your belief might swing in the
opposite direction. Examine this. Metamodernism is the idea that between
both of those ends of the pendulum of feeling, beliefs and ideas there exists
truth - or this is how I interpret the idea. Between our extreme polarity,
truth exists within suspended space of our feelings and perception of the
world. You may not believe that truth is absolute - whereas, the opposing
end of that belief is the idea that there is absolute truth. And somewhere
within your feeling exist the truth.

Fact/Feeling Both/And

If we choose our feelings over facts, we discredit the very structure of feeling. Whereas, feeling should be informed by facts. If we lead our assumptions about life and the world through a lens of feeling, we disregard reality. Metamodernism seeks to make sense of our feelings by applying structure to the feelings we experience in this polarity of culture.

Our feelings are swayed back and forth, and to grasp any kind of sense within chaos. So we have individuals who are led to inform their worldview through a sense of feelings within right and wrong, compassion and empathy but informed by desire to harness the internal chaos they emotionally experience from the external world of politics, religion, economics, globalization and technology. On the other end of the spectrum, we have those who inform their entire worldview through facts alone and discount the sense that feeling or empathy as a result of those facts, or informed by the facts are not something to take into account.

What I am proposing here is that both fact and feeling can exist simultaneously and that truth may lie within the existence of both. However, the hinge of an individual existence on feeling or fact alone may be a dangerous path that results in Marxism, Authoritarianism or Totalitarianism ideas to an extreme. It is not to say that the intention of those who speak truth through either narrative desire these outcomes, but that those who choose a side of the pendulum for interpretation may not be equipped to make sense of the message and choose to exist within the extreme. Politically speaking, we can see this example through far left protests and Antifa movements to the Alt-Right movements in support of Trump. The facts, or lack of facts, inform the feeling and the over abundance of feeling dismiss the desire for facts.

We have created extreme polarities.

"In 2010, cultural theorists Timotheus Vermeulen and Robin van den Akker proposed metamodernism as an intervention in the post-postmodernism debate In their essay Notes on Metamodernism, they asserted that the 2000s were characterized by the return of typically modern positions that did not forfeit the postmodern mindsets of the 1980s and 1990s, resembling a "neo-romanticism" represented especially in the work of young visual artists. According to them, the metamodern sensibility "can be conceived of as a kind of informed naivety, a pragmatic idealism", characteristic of cultural responses to recent global events such as climate change, the financial crisis, political instability, and the digital revolution. They asserted that "the postmodern culture of relativism, irony, and pastiche" is over, having been replaced by a post-ideological condition that stresses engagement, affect, and storytelling." ("Metamodernism", 2020)

Metamodernism creates an emotional framework in which we can understand the future of ourselves and the future of humanity. A progression beyond the postmodern and a reimagining of modernism to exist where both are valid with each other. Within this sense of polarity, the emotional state of humanity will oscillate between sincerity and irony.

The cultural paradigms that have driven pop culture for the past 60 years will now be recognized as existing at once. And this is where we are headed. We are at the precipice of this feeling, yet this idea is not yet mainstream. It is moreso at the phase of when Nirvana was playing music in a garage before anyone knew who they were, or when Steve Jobs and Wozniak were building home computers before Apple, or when everyone thought Bezos was crazy for selling books on the internet. Metamodernism is murmuring through those garages and discussions online, but it is not yet mainstream.

However, this is important to recognize and understand from a design perspective because we must have an ability to think, create, imagine and build beyond our own perceptions and inform the decisions within our work through a perception of others as we design solutions for larger impact. As we move forward into a more globalized world economy and culture, the impact of our work becomes much more important. If we desire to have a seat at the leadership table, to contribute in meaningful ways, and design better solutions to the challenges we face that have created from either a modernist or postmodernist framework - we absolutely must look at the future where both modern and postmodern ideology exist and form some new path and approach for design. It is no longer relevant or sustainable to choose an approach of design built out of a modernist hierarchical form of work or a postmodernist form of work.

Design is about understanding humans. Without understanding humanity or culture, design inherently falls apart. Design is creating solutions for humanity at various degrees to forge ahead, build new solutions, and create a better world.

Steve Jobs understood this.

He had a clear understanding of the world, humanity and what people needed - beyond what they realized they needed. His fervent and adamant decisions about how the products of Apple should look and feel was deeply embedded within his own opinions, and those opinions were formed by his understanding of humanity.

Those who try to emulate Jobs without having a perspective of humanity will fail. I believe this to be true with all great leaders who have innovated and moved us forward in our lifetime. The "what" and "how" is not what is to be replicated, but to understand their "why" and how this belief informs their drive to create through a deep understanding and perceptive of humanity beyond themselves.

I believe men like Gates, Musk, Ford, Carnegie, Rockefeller and Jobs all understood this about themselves and the calling to move civilization forward. In essence, today we are witnessing those who have a desire to be the "Hero" like these icons by way of imitation. The engineers of Silicon Valley are not revolutionists, the startup founders creating social media apps for segments of our population by way of identity are not innovators, the disruptors of culture by way of art, music or fashion are reusing styles and mediums informed by sub-cultures from three decades ago.

The courage to innovate and move forward into the future is not built on the pursuit of riding the coattails of being the next startup founder, IPO-ing another mobile app or disrupting an industry. This is not innovation.

Those who choose to innovate and create industries that did not exist a few decades ago did so without the help of investors, backers, a full stack development team, speaking on panels, and the unending rounds of "networking" so evident in the innovation spaces we see today. These innovators built ideas from nothing with little-to-no-funding driven by a vision and a belief that informed their drive to create deeper than a desire to be significant, or relevant, or the "Hero" of humanity's story. They sought to design and create a better world. Our society has become informed by the vision's of those innovators. And the pursuit of trying to create the next Twitter-esque-Facebook-style-social-media-app-mixed-with-some-other-form-of-bullshit is not the path of innovation - and those who pursue these ideas are nothing more than snake oil salesman. They are not innovators.

I implore a new call to action. To look at the world from a different perspective and consider the future landscape existing between both modern and postmodernism. To unpack and understand where you personally exist within that paradigm and use that understanding to define, imagine, create and innovate new forms of ideas for society well beyond the current structure built through either a modernist or post-modernist perspective. Not to discredit either the great minds of modernism or post-modernism - but to step back and look at the path we are heading towards, and see a new opportunity to design a future built upon different understandings and places to consider where new innovations for humanity can exist. To utilize the current structure, connectivity, and globalization of our world to build something outside of the narratives we are currently trapped within. To liberate humanity at the individual level. To give people hope by designing new ideas where they can discover their own truth and belief about their own existence. To define and make sense of their own meaning and purpose. Beyond the current structure of our work building into the sincerity or irony of it all.

I believe the next place of innovation is the understanding of human thought and emotion at a global level. Capturing the needs, desires, fears and drive of humans and using this information to inform the next version of humanity. The polarity in which we exist today is divisive in nature. It does nothing to further our progress, but only creates continued wedges between a far left and far right ideology rooted in either modern and postmodern foundations. I believe that the future will shift to understand that their is value in both a modernist approach to the progress of man and the hierarchy of systems combined with the irony rooted within postmodern ideals. Where both exist. Until the understanding of this feeling is actualized at a mainstream level, we will continue to choose either/or and spin in our various circles of identity and decision to be one or the other.

The alternative is that we, as designers, look at our world, consider the future and make a decision about the space between both modern and postmodern. Where we can choose to find the space between the polarity of the pendulum, where truth resides. And this can inform our approach to our work, to build from this foundation, and to seek to design a new world beyond the extremity of emotions from either modern sincerity or post-modern irony - and choose to intentionally create from the metamodern place of both-and.

Creating from this metamodern place allows the designer to truly de-sign for humans.

Design is a pursuit of creating a better world. As the tensions and os-cillation between economics, global crises, pandemics, disease, political movements, policies, war, religion, and culture; we become more intercon-nected than ever before. Yet the chaos and confusion within the individual existing in a global environment brings an intensity of understanding the self to a place where humanity has never experienced before.

If we seek to design a better world and create better solutions, we must have a perspective about the state of humanity that far exceeds the micro-details of each design element within our work. We should exist within the tiniest of details and the global impact our work has for future generations.

Design is solving challenges. Metamodernism presents emotional chal-lenges, but within this I believe there is a new emergence of design and an approach that creates a profound opportunity. To design new and emerging ideas where we intentionally embrace both modernism and postmodernism within our work to allow for the audience to exist between both. Therefore allowing the audience to discover meaning and truth within themselves through our design efforts.

Modernism was intentionally designed. The frameworks and structures that built civilization was an effort of design through business, architecture, industrialization and the rise of mankind.

Post modernism is also designed. The rebellion against the modernist, the disruption of the status quo, the angst against the injustices of the world are all facets of postmodernism that are intentionally created as a form of disruption.

Both of these sensibilities have been designed and created within culture by humans.

If we aspire to heal the world through design and solve challenges at global levels. We must recognize that since postmodernism is the status quo, it will not be for much longer - and the next step within the current framework of the world is where both modern and postmodern sensibilities exist simultaneously.

As a designer, we should not hinge ourselves within one ideology or the other.

We must not be a modernist designer or a postmodernist designer.

The cultural and political aspects of these ideologies have bombarded the design and tech industries. And the continuation of the path is going to lead to irrelevance or at worst, self destruction.

We must evolve as designers and throw away the idea of subscribing to a ideology. The only way we can design for the future where both paradigms exist, is to recognize the polarity of metamodernism within the individual self before we can aspire to solve challenges for the world through design.

This book outlines my thoughts about how the future designer should approach their work, their well-being and venture into preparation for the next iteration of what a designer is going to represent for the world.

The importance of understanding cultural shifts through a design lens.

We must be more aware of the world and our place in the world if we seek to design for the future.

We must adapt and evolve in our practice of design to become leaders in culture and business.

We need to see beyond the client-service relationship and understand that the intentions of our design efforts inform the type of world we have created, and also the type of world we can nurture in the future.

Who we are as an individual within the construct of a growing connected global world becomes important as our work becomes informed by both modern and postmodern ideals.

If we choose stay within one side our work will be ineffective and irrelevant.

We see this today where startups and creators are trying to make new ideas, platforms or services that are remixes of what already exists. This is not creativity. This is postmodern ideology influencing an approach that lacks vision or innovation. The next version of innovation will exist in creating platforms and services where the audience experiences an intentional effort of both modern and postmodern approaches without the baggage of political or cultural influence. Tto then discover meaning within themselves to awaken and understand truth.

Designing a better world through a metamodern lens means designing a better experience beyond political influence, profit driven efforts, lifestyle brands, capitalism disguised in greenwashing or embedded narratives within entertainment. We must consider new ways to create a human experience that allows the space between the modern and postmodern to be designed. In order to do this, we must first look at ourselves as designers. We must understand our own intentions and identify that feeling between modernism and postmodernism before we can consider designing the future.

The approach of design through a metamodern lens is not to embrace "both-and" and decide for our audience how they should feel and interpret our work, but to balance our work with "both-and" so that our audience can emotionally exist between the polarity of sincerity and irony to feel a sense of tension and decide for themselves what truth lies within the oscillation of our work, and in turn develop a sense of truth about the world.

Therefore, I believe that the future of design is built upon a new approach of the individual designer in order to approach our work differently.

My efforts here are to outline this approach through not only our work, but through the development of a new lens of design in which we can observe both the modern and postmodern ideals that simultaneously exists within the world. And in turn, our job is to not decide through our work, but to present an evolved approach of our work in order to help humanity understand themselves at the individual level, beyond the decision to choose between the opposing sides of the pendulum of culture. To allow our audience a new solution which exists between "both-and" to choose and decipher truth for themselves, beyond the existing narrative - to design for a grand narrative.

Continuing the current path of design has consequences

The alternative to continuing this path we are on places design within the oscillating pendulum of society. If we choose to continue to exist at the current pace of design and the design industry, we will face a continued path of diminishing relevance and lack of leadership within larger design challenges.

We must practice new concepts within our work and seek to look at the whole of society and culture beyond our own perceptions. Our beliefs about the world through the lens of tradition or disruption should be challenged to where we can see both sides to inform a new approach of finding "both-and" within our work. The continuation of false narratives perpetuate the information of cultural narratives and design exists as a tool to continue this narrative. We are a commodity to a greater narrative of falsehoods from both perspectives of society - both embedded with ulterior motives, hidden agendas and a pursuit for ultimate power and control. And yet, design exists as a tool to promote the individual self for meaning and purpose applied to a greater good that is ultimately driven by narratives which may or may not be true.

We must seek to approach our work differently as to think beyond choosing a side, or fighting against the opposition, but to use design to build a better future through our decisions out of a new perspective for our work. Beyond the mindset of "either/or" and encased in an ideal of "both-and". If we seek truth within our work, and purpose within our decisions, we must step back, look at our own individual views and seek to exist within "both-and" to build new and innovative solutions moving forward. If not, we will continue toward a path of chaos where we oscillate every few years between market changes, corporate earnings, political elections and the 24-hour news cycle of being victim to our own creations.

The design of society is set between the chaos and we have built a landscape of confusion and misinformation only to swing the pendulum back and forth hoping that some sort of truth will come out of the emotional battle - but this pendulum swing will continue to grow wider and wider. We will see a growing sense of depression, mental health and suicidal rates increase. Because humanity was not meant to fall victim to a chaotic narrative and disorder, but to define meaning and purpose for the individual self.

I believe it is the job of designer's to bear this burden with great concern and reconcile with the individual responsibility that we have in our work and it's ripple-effect and impact we choose to put into the world. There is no peace within the continued battle for right and wrong in our current cultural approach. The back and forth rebuttals are fighting for relevancy at the expense of designing human narratives at polar extremes. We must step back and re-evaluate this on the individual, cultural and global landscape if design will be a tool for good in the future. If we choose to ignore this path and pattern, we could be contributing to civilizations greatest depression, ourselves. And we bear the responsibility of placing us on that path, but we also can choose to take a new approach for a brighter future.

Modernism builds.

Post modernism deconstructs.

Metamodernism reconstructs.

Where others mistake defining metamodernism is the outcome of examples, I view metamodernism as the intention that drives the outcome. Simply pointing to the example as embracing "oth-and" while dismissing examples where the intention and outcome are both-and is where I differ on other opinions of metamodernism.

My definition of examining not only the outcome and intent, my exploration of "both-and" from and internal and external lens of metamodernism has led me through a personal path of reconstruction where intention, truth, faith and ideologies have shifted.

For example, my personal journey of metamodernism has embraced outcomes and ideas that may be right leaning in modern stereotypical archetypes and tropes, but the feeling about them derived from a "both-and" internal framework of exploration . Through my journey, conservative foundations such as truth, faith, a higher purpose, God, hunting for my own food, importance of family and hard work exist as values along with the part of myself that values disruption, rebellion (of pop culture mainstream media), mindfulness, consciousness, science, reason and questioning the status quo. Both exist and hold value within my understanding of the world. Metamodernism is not a tool to secretly leverage a leftist ideology. Nor is it a tool to dismantle a traditional conservative ideology. It is the expansive examination of both ancient truth born from centuries of the human story and the unknown future in which we must create, imagine and progress towards.

My explorations in these writings examine a future of design related to the ancient truths of our human story combined with a vision of an evolved framework in which we could approach design. And it encompasses a view in which the ideals of design apply not only to those who wear a title of design or creative within the present world, but a call that this design thinking can be valued among conscious leaders, visionaries and builders of our future across all disciplines.

If design is everything and everything is design, then all humans embody design and are designers.

The Future of Brands and Business

—

We have differing views of what a brand is. Those who work within the landscape of branding have differing thoughts. Those who design for brands may see it as the expression through visual or marketing or identity efforts, and those who experience brands think of it as the end-consumer experience. The definitions are wide and broad.

A brand exists much deeper than the expression. It is the combination of understanding the purpose, vision, mission and values of a business and embraced by those who run the business and understood by the audience who experiences those attributes. It is then up to the audience to determine how they feel about those ideals. The feeling about those ideals from the audience is what the brand actually is. The roles of messaging, marketing, communication, advertising, social media, logo, identifies, photography, film, broadcast are all efforts for the brand to support and reinforce their continued beliefs about their purpose, vision, mission and values to their audience. The consistency in those experiences related to the makeup of the brand identity determines the effectiveness and impact that a brand has on their audience.

The brands that understand this build a brand that plays a role within the audience's own journey. They exist to help them along their journey beyond their own expression through products, services, marketing and advertising efforts. This is a human-centered empathy driven approach to build a brand. As consumers are becoming smarter and better at understanding their roles within a brand - they want to participate. The company and customer make up the brand as a community or tribe of people who hold a shared value system and are along for a continued journey.

Brands of the future will need to integrate their business practices, understanding of their audience and goals to achieve their purpose, vision, mission and values in new ways. The single-line of communication is gone. The two-way channel of communication is the current landscape and brands are trying to engage and capitalize on this. But the future will be a community of people holding a shared set of valued defining and evolving the brand from the consumer side more heavily. Holding true to a companies purpose, vision, mission and values in the future will attract customers and allow them the space to continue to evolve and help shape the brands of the future.

Greenwashing will make brands irrelevant. Advertising will cease to be effective. Trying to convince your audience through clever and witty marketing ideas will fail time and again. The Mad-Men style marketing, advertising, and creative dinosaurs of today will become extinct. The creative agencies will dry up. The power of the brand of the future will exist within a more sincere relationship between the company and the audience.

Revolutions change culture.

Culture changed during the postmodern movements in an attempt to break away from the modernist ideas of society.

Singular people impacted generations. Modernism built the world in which postmodernism has a voice.

Collective brands will lead the next revolution. A communal tribe of people joining together and allowing the audience to build and define the brand will be the next revolution.

Brand must evolve via metamodernism because the old tired ways of modernism are ineffective and the newness of postmodernism will soon wear off and consumers will grow tired of the postmodern approach to brands and business.

But brands cannot be seen going backward to modernist ideals because they have already spent their brand equity on nostalgia through a postmodern lens. The only option is to move forward and if forward looks like choosing modernism or postmodernism, the brand will essentially be fighting an uphill battle and lose half of their audience. This is about the audience, the customer, the consumer, the person on the other end experiencing the brand. They will be the ones to control the narrative of a brand. They will be the ones to build and determine the value of the brand.

The modernist approach of one-way communication and ideals through marketing and advertising will no longer work - and in fact may alienate a brand who continues this route. The alternative disruptive approach through the lens of postmodernism will fall of deaf ears of the consumer as they have evolved beyond the tactics of a business. The audience wants more. They want to feel. They want to be heard and contribute in meaningful ways. If they cannot create, they want to consume in ways that define their own purpose and meaning.

Metamodernism is a vehicle to create power and opportunity for the audience to decide for themselves the value of brand or business similar to the way someone may experience and decide the value of a painting in an art gallery or the new indie rock band they discovered in a record store. When you allow the audience to sift through their feelings and make a decision about how they can and should feel without selling them anything other than an experience, you create a new way for communicating value beyond the tired old tactics.

The current problem exists because we live in a hierarchical societal order. Whether you like hierarchy or not - it exists. It's a natural occurring state of humans that has been around since the beginning of time. If you aren't going to change the hierarchy, you must wait it out or take your turn when it comes. If not, you must look for new ways to explore.

In a world where humans are rapidly evolving within themselves, seeking strength within, building stronger identities, understanding their roles within a global and local society and becoming more in-tune with the internal feelings oscillating from the external world; it has created polarities within ourselves, our culture and our contributions to society as a whole. We are trying to make sense of our existence while being pulled in every direction to be told what to think, how to think and uncovering truths and discovering lies. The dominating factor of media, entertainment and content at every turn has created a world of massive advertising, messaging and a fight for attention. We are driven by consuming yet left feeling fulfilled by the pursuit of consuming. Brands constantly trying to sell us products, services or ideas without any responsibility of the outcome or effects.

Brands are continuously fighting for attention. Fast following technology and trends and adopting campaigns to fit within the time and space. This resonates as insincere to an evolving human race who is seeking to make sense of their own existence, yet find themselves constantly bombarded by advertisements and messaging from companies who solely seek to convince them of their loyalty without providing any truth beyond consumption. The alternative to this is a vast group of companies pivoting into greenwashing, doing good and standing on pillars of virtue without any accountability from their audience. It's a virtue signal in it's purest form.

Brands exist and compete against each other in a hierarchical construct. Against other brands. Fighting for the attention of the consumer. Some brands have built hierarchical power over time, with any inability to compete. See Apple, Disney, IBM, Google. All of these companies started out at one time or another as a postmodern pursuit to create change, fight the "powers that be" and throw a wrench into the modernist system. And they won, in the end. However, the postmodern approach that these brands held evolved into a modernist corporate company. They hire postmodern thinkers who must align to their modernist structures. Built around open workspaces, free coffee, ping-pong tables and work from home fridays. Yet, it is now modernism disguised as postmodernism. Lipstick on a pig. These companies are focused on the bottom line. What was once a passion to build a revolution has now turned into appeasing shareholders and lobbying the government.

Younger, postmodern brands exist in startups with funding, bootstrapping a new company online, or creating a lifestyle brand to attract those who are still hungry for some sort of revolution. Yet, these brands leave the audience unfulfilled. And we, as humans, oscillate between the megalith corporate entities who connect us to (almost) every living person on the plant, while still trying to fulfill our hungry yearning for progress through postmodern brands who sell on the idea of rebellion, irony and angst.

The sense of brand communication and brand relevance in the world leaves the audience empty. There is no fulfillment. There is a sense of missing the deepest emotions and complexities to truly be loyal to, well, anything.

Tactics of modernism dont work. The one-way communication model for brands related to marketing and advertising are ineffective and today borderline on manipulation and propaganda.

Tactics of postmodernism are worn out. We see the influence of post-modernism throughout mainstream entertainment, adopted by brands and experiences and informing our current landscape of media, entertainment and culture. However, this post-modernism was not always the mainstream and as history shows, that which is in the mainstream will fade and we move toward something else.

Humans are actively seeking substance. The approaches that brands have today are becoming worn out, ineffective and we have grown to become less optimistic about experiencing brands in digital and experiential forms. The next version of our engagement with technology will exist in a less optimistic way as we yearn for more meaning and substance within our own lives, beyond what brands and media are telling us how and what we should believe and consume in our personal lives.

Why is this relevant to brands in the future?

The world has rapidly changed. We exist in a complex technologically advanced world. And the future of business and brands will be more impacted by the influence of design, design strategy and design thinking around an approach where the evolution of branding is going to evolve with the evolution of consumer habits and expectations.

Best case scenario: brands play a more humanity driven role and define their purpose. They begin to humanize their business where sincerity, vulnerability and honesty are at the forefront combined with the playfulness of irony and self awareness of their own existence within the lives of their audience.

Worst case scenario: Brands play to far into the oscillating extremes of their own identity without the balance combined with execution and strategy and it polarizes their brand into controversial, non-impactful, and a lack of sincerity as the undercurrent of their survival.

There is a deeper yearning for purpose, substance, understanding of one's own role in a global society. Technology has connected us in meaningful ways, yet we feel more lonely than ever before. We are seeking depth and engagement to understand ourselves through the lens of a greater purpose and call to the betterment of humanity.

Oscillation between modernism and post-modernism has been emerging since the 1970's, though we have witnessed the influence and acceleration over the past decade. We have sought to try and find and define meaning through supporting products and services that directly communicate with us in, what is now, archaic messages. We have been accepting of one-way dialogue and messaging. We have been conditioned to accept everything as a sales-pitch. Since the advertising days of Mad Men to the angsty cultural revolution of MTV.

The future of brand and business relies on our ability to take action now related to our own responsibility, ethics and design of a future in which we envision. We must seek to impact our audience first, build brand loyalty and connect to create a lasting relationship in honest and transparent ways. To build meaningful brands of the future, we must deliberately and intentional create a higher sense of purpose within ourselves, our business and express this to our audience. ROI will not be an impact of clicks, likes, follows and clever campaigns, but through long term audience engagement as we guide them on their own journey of life. Through open, honest dialogue, we are building deeper substance and meaning that reflects through our purpose translated first through engagement and secondly through our product or service.

The challenge of this approach is that it is a long-term plan that can be difficult to execute once the strategy is in place. Organizational changes may occur, priorities may shift, competitors may arise, the cultural landscape may change, uncertainty will happen. However, the foundations built in thoughtful brand strategy will help to guide the business and weather storms far beyond the constant chase of trends, relevancy, campaigns, advertisements and marketing efforts. This shift is coming and you either embrace and adapt or you watch your audience fulfill their meaning and purpose through other companies and organizations who "get it".

Brands during the modernist movement were giant ominous figures. Brands in the post-modernist movement were young angsty reckless indie companies tearing away at the modernist corporate behemoths. However, the future of branding exists where the barriers between customer and company will deteriorate. Customers will exists as an interactive and integral audience member on the brand stage.

A collective eco-system of people helping the brand to build greater good in the world. This eco-system will exist collaboratively, transparently and require contribution from the audience, business and all humans involved within the brand experience.

An extension of the humans involved within the brand as employees, and simultaneously an extension of the customers they serve. Barriers between the faceless brand, masked by logos, style guides and social media barriers will dissipate. Brand identities will be informed and shaped by the relationships between the company and humans. The future brand will care less about the brand image, the brand logo and the overall brand presentation and more about the experience in which they offer - the expression will inform but not lead.

A deeper value system will emerge for the audience. A brand must first identify their values and live through those beliefs. These values must consist of the people within the organization as a collective purpose and vision. The values must also be a realistic representation not just through a well-crafted mission statement, or a set of values hung in the office, but a true representation carried out through the actions of everyone involved with the brand. It will not be contrived, fake, misled or a feel good belief - but a true representation.

Brands will be more aware of their role within culture at both a global and local perspective. They will be sensitive and cognoscente of the impact they have both locally and globally from every aspect of their business - products, services, experiences and communication.

Brands will embrace vulnerability. They will celebrate their strengths and openly acknowledge their weaknesses and shortcomings. Being honest and transparent along this brand journey. They will stop pretending to be something they are not - both informed by modern and post-modern ideals, because the interactions with their audience will not need convincing. The audience is now highly evolved and smarter than the tactics we have been conditioned to from decades of marketing and advertising. Be exist beyond.

Brands will seek to be more playful without fear of losing their own face-value. They will take on the idea of not taking themselves so seriously. There will exist a proper balance of playfulness related to the inherent DNA and archetypes of the brand.

Brands will exist as a platform and community for conversation, connection and growth. Open dialogue will be accepted and welcomed. Conversation will engaged between the audience, the community and the brand itself. A brand's responsibility in the future will focus on connecting with humans in an open and transparent way. The face of the brand will be less about the logo and identity and more about the human to human experience. The experience will help the audience grow, learn, explore and discover new ways to define their own humanity. The brand will work as the guide.

Brands will be more transparent in their mission, vision and operations. There will be an expectation far beyond the current state of "greenwashing" where these beliefs carried out through action will be transparent and open-sourced.

Brands of the future will be focused less on selling a product or service, but equally important, the will focus on their contributions to society and how they can help and encourage their audience to grow individually through the brand experience and guidance. The products or services will help them accomplish a greater sense of self. The focus of brand communication will shift from selling through marketing and advertising to education, guidance and human connection.

A brand will exist as an ever-changing and evolving organism representing a culture, system and business of people who have come together to sell a product or service. They will no longer have customers. They will have audiences. Every person will be a potential customer will always be a human audience members, a part of the community, first and foremost. With so many choices to find a product or service, a brand's impact will be how they engage with their audience. The engagement must be real, tangible and seeking to break down barriers of traditional branding through technology, media and advertising. Humanity will come to the forefront. Helping others without the intent to sell, but the intent to grow.

Humanity will greatly benefit from this paradigm shift of brand and business. However, those who still support the polarizing oscillating extremes of either modernism or post-modernism will be harmed. They will still emotionally exist within a space where the ideals, politics, and global beliefs a brand from the old-world represents will need to be articulated beyond their current mindset. The uncomfortable fear of personal growth, uncertainty and self-discovery is polarizing within itself and this shift will emerge deep fears from those who exist within the polar extremes we see today in society.

The choice to make this shift is at the helm of thought leaders, visionaries, designers, leaders, executives and cultural tastemakers. They can positively prepare and impact the future of humanity at both a local and global level by recognizing the need for change within the internal culture of a business or organization combined with deeply understanding the emotional needs of the audience beyond a product or service.

Leadership and creatives will be the key pioneers of this movement. Those who are brave enough to see the long-term benefits, the path of culture and society combined with the courage to make a shift into the future of their own business. They must reflect on the honest representation of their own self and break away from examples of corporate brands trying to perceived as young and hip, or early startups trying to feel nostalgic.

Brands will be expected to grow, mature, evolve, celebrate their successes, and be open about their weaknesses. Pivoting on campaigns to appear relevant, conscious, political, or activist in various ways will fall flat. Brands must use their voice in appropriate ways without the intention to distort, diminish, or deceive the audience through traditional communication methods. We dont need corporations trying to speak to millennials like they are hip and with it. It's insulting. We don't need new brands playing into the post-modern ways of reckless angst to be cool. Brands must step back and really be honest with themselves about who they are. Their strengths and weaknesses are not defined by themselves, but by their audience. The audience is not necessarily a customer, but a cultural observer to the brand's interaction within the world.

Throughout history, businesses, companies and organizations have evolved and changed to be effective and impactful by promoting their image to a consumer with the intention of selling something. That something might be a product or a service or a way of thinking. In any case, the goal within the modernist and post-modern movements was to buy something or become anti-that-something and seek to buy something that was the counterculture of that thing we were being sold.

Brands of the future will need to develop massive self-awareness. Intentional brands will be effective and influential. Creative execution within irony and sincerity will emerge as it creates a deeper sentiment for the audience to engage emotionally with the brand - building loyalty and brand equity.

Small to medium sized brands will be able to pivot quickly, take risks and adapt to change that will disrupt. As we watch the struggle of the current SP500 companies, the infusion of capital from the Federal Government to keep large businesses afloat, we witness the opportunity emerging each day where small to medium sized companies who have a long-term thoughtful outlook on the future of humanity can develop long-term strategy that takes their own relevancy beyond the traditional business models to sustain long term growth, emotional connection and the ability to weather financial disaster.

How should brands approach this safely?

Strategy

Brands need to build a solid foundation of who they are, who their audiences are and work endlessly to understand both. A brand needs to understand themselves through an open and honest lens where they recognize their strengths and weaknesses without trying to be something they are not.

A brand needs to identify and understand their audiences(s) at a deeper level. What do they care about? What drives them? What are their needs and what is their purpose and meaning in life? This extends far greater than demographics and psychographics and arbitrary data about a user group. Knowing the emotional needs and purpose of your audience will help you find alignment between your brand values and their values. From here, you can begin to communicate effectively.

Both / And

Brands have hinged themselves into a group of attributes. They create positioning statements and lead with these attributes to propel themselves into the future. However, metamodernism is about "both-and", whereas the brand attributes must also encompass the polarity of those attributes. A brand must seek to address and examine the opposing attributes that which they do not obtain. A brand must utilize the opposing attributes in balance to their intention and execution. Creating a balance of the brand and causing an oscillation with the audience. This oscillation creates a tension within the audience and allows the audience to decide on their own feelings.

This deciding factor is outside of both modernism and post-modernism. Where the messaging has previously been strategic, decided upon, given a focused outcome and targeted to a desired measurable state with a wide array of personas within an audience. Metamodernism approaches this differently, saying "both-and". Where the audience is left to decide and make sense of their own feelings.

Executed in balance, th tension creates a sense of feeling with the audience that encompasses a broader worldview in their own lives and allows that feeling to also resonate, in whatever way it may, with the brand message. This "both-and" approach is unconventional from decades of studying brands, measurable outcomes and desired effects, however, given the landscape and the future of our culture, both globally and locally, brands of the future will need to address this sense to connect with audiences at a deeper, more meaningful place. A brand of the future contains depth, complexity, pastiche and light-heartedness all wrapped into a single experience - or oscillating various experiences to the audience.

"The metamodern structure of feeling evokes an oscillation between a modern desire for sens and a postmodern doubt about the sense of it all, between a modern sincerity and a postmodern irony, between hope and melancholy and empathy and apathy and unity and plurality and purity and corruption and naïveté and knowingness; between control and commons and craftsmanship and conceptualism and pragmatism and utopianism. Indeed, metamodernism is an oscillation. It is the dynamic by which it expresses itself. One should be careful not to think of this oscillation as a balance however; rather it is a pendulum swinging between numerous, innumerable poles. Each time the metamodern enthusiasm swings towards fanaticism, gravity pulls it back towards irony; the moment its irony sways towards apathy, gravity pulls it back towards enthusiasm" ("Notes on Metamodernism", 2010)

A shift in communication from a business will be important for the future sustainability of the brand. A focus on openness, honesty, transparency and humanity will be driving force of vulnerability from those who operate the business. The messaging and tone will be a blended mix of sincerity and irony. Mapping the messaging to real values while balancing the polarity of both sincerity and irony within the brand expression. For example: The Gillette ad that focused on toxic masculinity was a politically driven ad rooted in sincerity and it fell flat. Car commercials take a sincere approach to their new vehicle and it feels old and reused. Gieco hinges on the comedy of their advertisements but miss on creating trust and deeper value. Super Bowl advertisements are the most watched and viewed where nothing is taken seriously whether they are either sincere or ironic in nature - because the medium in which they exist has become a cultural trope.

Discover new mediums to engaged the deeper communication and the ironic communication. Podcasts, long form content, social media, commercials and advertisements are tactics in which the balance of sincerity and irony can exist in content, context and expression.

The expression should visually balance the polarity of sincerity and irony. Sincere intent with ironic execution though tone, colors, photography, film and visual expression. Or an ironic intent with sincere execution through tone, colors, photography, film and visual expression. The balance within the execution allows the audience to feel different, to take on the feeling for themselves and decide how they want to feel at various touchpoints of the brand. Visual expression and messaging balance the polarity of both sincerity and irony. Sincere visual with ironic messaging, or, ironic visual with sincerity messaging.

A new creative approach will emerge where sincerity and irony will simultaneously exist within the visual expression. The intentional balance between visual, audio, film, creative and messaging combined with the intentional balance of sincerity and irony to create new works. This will give a sense of tension within the work to allow the audience to decide how they should feel, an inverse effect of how traditional advertisements and marketing is designed to effect the consumer. Traditional creative briefs hinge on the intentional outcome of a feeling - warm, inviting, hopeful, funny, rugged, empowering, adventurous, magical, etc. New creative will exist to pair a tension between creative efforts within a work to allow the audience to decide how they should feel within the experience. Art direction and creative direction should seek to balance the creative efforts.

How does this benefit the business?

A brand of the future will develop more self-awareness. It will better serve the employees, because the sense of purpose and meaning within the company is not built within the hierarchical structure of the business, or the lackthereof as a post-modern experiment. A brand willing to accept that both hierarchy and post-modernism both have their place in the values of the company create an oscillation within that will resonate out. The business does not become an echo chamber but a place to explore and balance within it's own oscillation of brand attributes. The business must accept that there are benefits from both a modern and post-modern philosophies By shifting the brand to internal employee development and focusing on better personal development for the audience, the brand can utilize both modern and post-modern approaches By recreating processes within the business, a brand can evolve into new ways by harnessing both modern and post-modern philosophies

As society evolves and humans understand the polarity of their individual impact on a local and global scale, a brand must also evolve to understand their impact. The future of consumers will shift from deciding to spend money to embracing and connecting with humans are various touch-points. How can we evolve and change with this knowledge for our own good? If we look at the cultural landscape and accept that their exists cultural extremes that oscillate from our current human experience both anchored in modernism and post-modernism ideals, and we can agree that the term "metamodernism" is a way to capture the feeling where the tension between both exists of not "either/or" but "both/and", then we can start to make sense of what the future might look like. And we can start to better design this future knowing that this feeling has emerged from local, global, technological advancements, politics, religion and economic shifts within the past decade. And it's not slowing down. We can embrace this idea and create open dialogue. We can seek to understand this ever changing landscape and evolution of the human condition.

Marketing campaigns will drastically change. If an ironic commercial is meant to make people laugh with the intent to sell the brand but shows no sign of vulnerability, the campaign will have little impact. If the campaign is hinged on beautiful over-dramatic imagery and messaging to evoke an emotion, it will fall flat. We are pulled in these various feelings constantly. Our guard is up. Our radars are fine tuned and we won't buy it anymore. There needs to be a balance of both irony and sincerity within a brand's voice. Depth and substance over 30 second ads. Tapping into the values and ethos of a brand cannot be fully communicated within traditional media. It tries, but will come across as insincere even though the intention is sincere. It will cease to have impact. Long form continuous dialogue will build upon the emotion of sincerity. Short-form dialogue will create opportunities of irony. Both must exist for a brand to build a deeper connection with the audience and allow them to decide how they should feel about the brand. Podcasts, editorials, books, documentaries all exists as meaningful places to be sincere - combined with short form advertisements, videos and comedy sketches to build upon the irony of the business and their own self-awareness.

Geico is a great example of brand who embraces the short-form irony, however they lack long-form sincerity. Joe Rogan is a great example of metamodernism in the sense that he has long form sincere podcasts combined with a stand-up routine with short form ironic jokes about culture.

The future will exist for brands who focus on serving the values and ethos of the customer without the intent of selling. The future of brands will engage in sincerity and irony in communicating these values. Simultaneously being vulnerable, open and honest while being aware enough to ensure there is irony in the message, the communication and the engagement of the audience.

Business of the future should empower their audiences to be revolutionaries. For themselves. For their community. And for the world. Business should advocate for open dialogue and true transparency. To allow the audience to create the brand experience along with the business. Doing good in the world, having a greater purpose and living through that purpose with a vision and mission will not be a selling point in the future. It will be an expectation that is observed, measured and evaluated from consumers. Any hint of disingenuous practice, alternative perceptions or lack of transparency will be an emotional signal to break ties with a business. The future brand will adopt the value of serving others over selling products.

Design strategy to clarify, focus, prototype, test, and revise every aspect of their living brand through products and services

Metamodern Strategy:

1. Honesty: The sincerity of our work, the intention behind the work being sincere and honest. The messaging and delivering of the output of our work being rooted in honesty.

2. Vulnerability: The intention to create a deeper sensibility of humanity within our work.

3. Humanity: To create new ways to allow our audience to experience sensibilities where modernism and post-modernism can both exist within our work.

4. Creativity: Approaching new creativity beyond the modern or post-modern approach.

5. Design-led: Putting the foundations of design at the forefront of our initiatives in business and brand at both local and global levels.

Execution:

1. The anti-brand: To be a brand that exists outside or beyond the current expectations of what a brand is today.

2. Faceless yet human: To be a corporate faceless behemoth that is humanized and incredibly personal.

3. Sincerity and irony: To embrace both sincerity and irony in a combination of work, or to oscillate between the two in various mediums.

Traditional media will be obsolete

The formulaic approach to advertising, marketing and driving business will cease to be effective. If the overall goal is to sell you a product or service, you will fail. We as humans are evolving within ourselves. Seeking internal strength. Seeking our internal revolutions. Seeking growth in mental, physical and spiritual wellness. We expect our brands and companies we support to do the same. We expect these companies to be an extension of the values we believe in. We expect the brands and the people who work for those brands to understand us at deeper levels than demographics, psychographics and data. We expect to grow as humans and we expect the brands and companies within our lives to grow as well.

Going green. Sustainability. Giving back. Donating proceeds. These are all tactics to align with a certain ethos, but these will be expectations without question in the future. Brands will not be able to market and advertise on these sentiments as humans evolve. We will expect that companies and businesses do their part in the world because they are ran, owned and operated by humans.

Brands will need to take on a more human form of

identity

The modernist approach of ominous brands formed under "Co." endings shrouded with Helvetica bold typography will cease to be effective. The post-modern brands hinging identity on reckless, rebellious, nostalgic and carefree business will be seen as childish and angsty. There needs to be a balance. Brands cannot mature as humans do in a way where they constantly shift and pivot to stay relevant. Brands must seek to evolve internally the way humans are evolving internally today. Fill the empty hole within the brand as an organism that serves to reflect the ethos and values of the company. Humans are complex, full of emotions - brands need to be complex and not trendy.

Stop selling

The future of branding must focus on development and less about selling a product or service. The product or service will be secondary to the values of the company. With the over-abundance of content, data, services, products and access - a successful brand will shift the focus from marketing and advertising with intent to sell, to share their story in a truly meaning way where sincerity and irony play integral parts to this story. Both need to be balanced and included. Lifestyle brands of today only tell half of this story. Hinging on overly dramatic or sincere approaches to their brand campaigns, with the subtle notion of trying to get people to adopt to their brand.

Our future role

"We're the middle children of history, man. No purpose or place. We have no Great War. No Great Depression. Our Great War's a spiritual war... our Great Depression is our lives. We've all been raised on television to believe that one day we'd all be millionaires, and movie gods, and rock stars. But we won't. And we're slowly learning that fact. And we're very,

very pissed off." Chuck Palahnuik, Fight Club

Our future role of business, brand and creators exist in deeply understanding our individual self before we approach having any impact within a business or brand. We need to address our own self-awareness, personal growth, mind, body, spirit and seek to find our own truth within the cultural oscillation of modernism and post-modernism. We should consider aligning with those who seek truth and support those who focus on love and making peace within the world. That being said, I believe there are some inherent truths that we have learned throughout ancient civilization where culture has abandoned these ideals en-masse.

The truth beyond the doctrinal differences of faith, where the church was the cultural epicenter of creativity dating back to ancient civilizations and seen around the world in art, architecture, sculptures and creativity, was once the inspiration for humanity.

I personally believe there will exist a resurgence of this idea to become the future epicenter for human creativity beyond the landscape of current brands, business and culture of today. I say this because as AI becomes more real, unemployment rates are growing, economic disaster is happening, pandemics are on the rise and all of these things are impacting humanity at global scales, humans will find a need to believe in something greater than themselves. To seek purpose. To find meaning. And to embrace this meaning as a human with the part of us that separates us from other species on Earth, the ability to create.

I believe that the old ways of religion will become irrelevant, in the sense of doctrines and dogma, and the truth of these ideals will emerge and inspire an exodus from the current cultural landscape. Not from choice, but of necessity. For humans to rediscover the self in which they have lost amidst the cultural expectations and polarities we have been conditioned to believe. We will seek to fill the hole in our soul and it will exist in a translational post-industrial digital-age that begins to capture the essence of humanity at a global level.

The workplace will embrace a purpose driven employee who will be activists, consumers will expect companies to take a stand for beliefs, communications will encompass a greater purpose and call to action, purpose-washing will be an idea of the past as it becomes the expectation, long form content will be a way to emotionally share and connect, experiential storytelling will provide a means for brands to express emotions and vulnerability while engaging the audience in a more emotionally driven-narrative.

How Might We Approach The Future of Design?

If the current landscape exists as grand narrative of metamodernism, how might we approach design in a thoughtful way to innovate and create better solutions for a seemingly oscillating world existing in a chaotic swinging of a cultural pendulum? How can we approach our work in new ways whereas design does not exist as a commodity, but as a cultural tool to innovate and imagine new ways for building a better humanity? Where do we go from this current place and understanding?

I believe that in order to evolve design and exist outside of the current paradigm we have created through the design of the internet, digital economy and global connectivity, we must revisit our own individual values and make sense of the self once again to form new perspectives and realign our approach to design.

The alternative is a continued downward spiral into the post-modern abyss of culture. We have seen the impacts of this narrative play out through history with less-than-ideal results.

We must commit, as designers, to understand ourselves and move forward into the future with a new perspective and approach about our role as the individual designer related to the global good and responsibility we must accept through our work.

These ideals are not only limited to our current ideas about the designer, but could be applied to all humans. Whereas, the existence of the "designer" for the future will not resemble the current landscape of the designer - as the current landscape does not resemble the "designer" from a few decades ago.

We must look at design from a global and local perspective. Work focused on the needs of our audience combined with an emphasis on the details are met with a global understanding and implications of our work as a ripple effect into culture, the future and our impact on society.

Design influences culture through new media, technology and branding.

MMXD: Metamodern Experience Design

—

Design recognizes patterns within society and builds upon successful patterns or strives to fix and improve patterns that may be broken. The idea of metamodernism in design is simultaneously looking at successful patterns and allowing the broken patterns to intentional create a sense of dissonance in our work. This intentional effort allows our work to be disruptive through intention and to exist as a new format of an experience where the audience not only experiences design, but they must also take on forms of design thinking within their own consciousness. We respect the audience as much as to allow them to make decisions beyond the old-world way of "knowing better" than them.

Steve Jobs had it right, during his time. To create work where he knew better than others and fought endlessly to create from that perspective. However, with the current landscape of global connectedness, because of his work (and Bill Gates, Zuckerberg, Bezos, etc). Our humanity now exists in a space of "what's next?" So as the evolution of design becomes a commodity to continue sustaining companies like Apple, Amazon, Facebook, etc who have profited off of the global connectedness, we find that many people feel isolated, alone, lost and wandering in their own sense of meaning and purpose. Therefore, our future efforts of design, recognized by this global oscillating pattern of sincerity and irony (defined as Metamodernism) seeks to create a further sense of self through recognizing and reframing the traditional patterns. Where we provide others the opportunity to feel a sense of discomfort and tension within the safety and security of their experiences, only to determine for themselves what the meaning and purpose of it all is - for them. Not us. Not Steve Jobs. We shift into a future outlook of design being intentional about the audience holding their own conclusions while we create new emotional platforms and experiences for them to sort through.

Recognizing patterns of this feeling in the arts, entertainment, music, politics, religion, global economics and more.

If we seek to intentionally create these new emotional platforms for our audience, I have defined a few key points to consider as a designer. Those exist currently as the below list, and may evolve, change, or be revised over time. But for now, this is where I see the opportunities of a designer leaning into the future of designing experiences with the intentional oscillation of both modernism and post-modernism.

Audience-centered narrative

Formulating the output of work, and also the intention of work from beginning of the process to end result as a consistent and conscious effort to focus solely on the needs of the audience. Where the intention is not based on what the Designer or business believes to be true, but to seek to explore and uncover the needs and desires of their audience and reflect this back to them in a compelling and creative way.

Unexpected vulnerability

Opportunities emerge to allow the intentional efforts on behalf of the audience to reflect vulnerability of the business and brand. What once was seen as a modernist protective environment within corporate culture will shift to a space of also allowing the weaknesses to be a place of conversation. Where the weaknesses come out of hiding, stop being swept under the corporate carpet and surface in true honesty. Not with the intention of selling a product, but to create new conversations because the old dialogue between business and customer is worn out - in both the modern and post-modern rhetoric. So we seek to explore and discover, intentionally, unexpected vulnerabilities that may emerge from both the business and the customer to create a new sense of belief, belonging and meaning within our work.

Meta-Interactive Design: Two forms of experience

Where we merge the intentional efforts we aspire from our users, customers, audience and boldly become self-aware of what our goals are. We blatantly and obviously profess these goals in a modernist approach while allowing the self-awareness of our own ambitions to come through in an ironic tone. The experience creates a new sensibility for our audience and allows them to decide how they should feel about the brand. "We are trying to sell you something and we aren't trying to be sneaky, clever or witty about it. We just want you to clearly by this thing and if you don't that's okay too."

Oscillation Design

Where we merge opposing sensibilities of modernism and post-modernism together. From both look and feel, with messaging and tone. We pair opposing modern and post-modern attributes to radically juxtaposition our brand. This creates a tension within our work, business and efforts and allows the audience to decide how they should feel about our brand and their connection to our brand. This removes the worn out approach of marketing from a corporate tone of "we know best" or the post-modern tone of "we are here to disrupt and be the rebel".

Everyperson Hero

The archetypes of society define personality traits around brands, businesses and celebrities. Whether we fully recognize this or not, we are drawn to opposing archetypes which will help us on our journey. Combine that with an overall effort of a brand or business related to a large customer base who all seeks a similar archetype, and you have a brand voice. The combination of a new kind of archetype exists where the personality takes on opposing archetypes. For example, The Everyperson is the Hero. We see this exemplified in norm core fashion with celebrities, Progressive Insurance commercials, indie films, and new consumer brands. We can find a relation between the desire to be a Hero, but find familiarity in a Hero who is an Everyperson. This is a juxtaposition of both the modernist Hero and the post-modernist Everyperson.

New Minimalism

Combining low level efforts of content, information, production value and creative with a larger grand narrative. This minimalism is meant to say more beyond the

Oscillation within the grand narrative

We either seek to combine the polarity of oscillating attributes of modernism and post-modernism to explore, discover or make sense of a grand narrative - or - we utilize the attributes of modernism and post-modernism combined to articulate a grand narrative.

Design Pastiche
UX / UI combinations

Merging of archaic design, computational design, skeuomorphism, ux/ui combinations where the feeling exists in both past computational design (early days of internet) combined with performance driven interaction, best practices and javascript. Or combining sleek modern design with clunky visuals of early days of the internet (think Yahoo! and GeoCities). Or the combination of design informed by natural aesthetic and organic materials mixed with the interaction of digital on mobile and desktop experiences.

Flat design vs. skeuomorphism

In digital, we see the movement of digital design trends shift from skeuomorphism (a realistic look to windows and buttons that feel tangible) to a radical shift into flat design over the past few years. We have shifted away from the usage of gradient buttons from the early 2000's into the 2010's of flat design being the norm. Prior to this, we experienced a clunky sort of web - not for lack of design, but for lack of synergy between design and development. The development of HTML and CSS was in it's infancy in the mid to late 90's and the hardware did not allow for large uses of javascript or high-res imagery to implement into design and a digital experience. Given the evolution of the web from this to Web 2.0 to where we are today, I see a resurgence of "digital nostalgia" coming, where we will revisit the influences and elements of the 90's digital design paired with really intelligent platforms, AI, mobile and reinvent through nostalgia a new experience in digital design. We will combine early 90s influences with flat design and skeuomorphism to create an entirely new feeling through digital.

Digital web design of the 90s was a result of post-modernists seeking to disrupt, envision a digital world and build upon the newness of the internet. I strongly remember the internet of the 90s where you had siloed websites, Yahoo, hotmail, AOL, ICQ messenger, a few large brands having a presence and a whole host of hobbyists creating on sites like GeoCities. The web was in its infancy. Born out the post-modernists vision of creating a global platform. People tinkered, designed, developed and built on top of existing platforms and languages to move us into Web 2.0 where we saw the rise of places like MySpace, Facebook and Silicon Valley startups.

This postmodernist approach to design and development was then given a new breathe of life when Apple began to pay attention to designing beautiful products and platforms. This infromed new developments, efforts, inspiration and ideas of what could now be capable with the evolution of the internet, browsers and experiences. The evolution grew from what felt like the future in the 90's but now looks like an archaic unfamiliar clunky past of the dial-up internet era. I see a nostalgic lean back into this sentiment to create new experiences that informed this culture of design and development from the 90s

Using expected design elements paired with other expected design elements that traditionally do not go together

Considering an approach to new ideas by combining elements from modernist movements and post-modern movements to create a tension within the work. Either from a place of visual or messaging encompassing the oscillating approach of modernism and post-modernism. New nostalgia that encompasses a futuristic approach to our work. Old modernism that is revamped to hold post-modern tonality. When we mix and match between modernism and post-modernism, we explore new sensibilities within the work combined with the intentions behind why the work was created. This pendulum builds new sensibilities for our audience in a metamodern approach.

Intentionally uninspiring

Normalcy of everyday life can emerge grand narratives. Choosing to discover the grand narratives and utilize everyday tools and objects to represent or define a greater meaning and be a useful tool for metamodern work.

Finding the grand narrative within the uninspiring parts of life builds an approach to our work that provokes deeper sensibility. To intentionally design an idea where the combination of a grand narrative is represented by an uninspiring idea or object creates an odd sense of tension for the audience.

Utilizing simple everyday tools and objects such as furniture, kitchen items, household products or office supplies to create or represent a grand narrative builds a new sensibility of these mundane items we often overlook or ignore. The balance is creating a grand narrative in our work with a post-modern tonality to oscillate between modernism and post-modernism.

For more inspiration here, I recommend reading "The Design of Everyday Things", Donald Norman or "The Psychology of Everyday Things", Donald Norman.

Metamodern Process

A process and strategy to move brands into the future using a metamodern approach to rethinking brands.

Understand the brand

Before we can evolve a brand, we must truly understand who the brand is, who they serve and what they do. From here, we can begin to build new pathways of creativity and design a new approach for the brand that exists within both modernism and post-modernism.

• Brand attributes: Culture of your brand, Feeling you want your audience to experience, Impact your brand has on your audience, Voice of your brand, X-Factor of what makes you unique

• Build brand positioning statement: A statement which defines who you are, what you stand for and who your audience is.

• Evaluate messaging from top 5 of each category: Build messages around the positioning statement and brand attributes.

• Map examples: Create examples and then rework them to find a balance between modernism and post-modernism tonalities.

All of these items being outlined, it is not to say that if you carry out these strategies and tactics, you will be a futuristic designer armed with new information and outlooks on your work to be cutting edge, radical and forward-thinking.

Not at all.

This is exists as the starting place.

The real effort lies within you, the Designer, the Business person, the

Creative, the driver of culture and society.

You must now embark on a deeper dive into the self. To understand and redefine where you must exist. Between the oscillation of both modernist and post-modernist ideals. Because truth does exist within one polarity or the other. And if you seek to guide others to an unwavering truth for themselves, you must understand this truth within yourself. Beyond your political, religious or bias leanings that you have learned over time. To think critically not about your work, but to think critically about your role and place within society and allow that understanding to effect and drive your work forward.

MMXD:
The Metamodern
Ex-Designer

—

When we recognize our role in the global and local landscape of design. Where we choose to understand our individual self applied to the greater global landscape while recognizing the insignificance and importance related to our local impact simultaneously. Culturally we must be hyper-observant of the local and global constructs in which society functions. Recognizing the value and risks of emerging tech that have both local and global positive and negative impacts. We must understand our individual role within these constructs and look through a lens where both the macro and micro observations help to guide our understanding of how we go about solving these challenges in the future.

A call to become the "Ex-Designer"

As the practice of design has become a commodity, I believe there will be a new iteration of design to emerge. Rooted in the self-awareness of the Designer within society, design will exist as a role which combines the practice and discipline of design mixed with the ability to observe and lead efforts through our changing globalization of culture. Understanding that design must be non-partisan, unbiased and focused on the core needs and desires of humanity at a level deeper than the current state of the design industry.

The discipline of design exists as a practice. However, in classical design, this practice existed in forms of letterpress, type, graphic design and print design. Along came the internet and computing and design transitioned to digital mediums. From here, we have seen a surge of design and availability of design tools to drive business and brands. But this over-saturation has diminished the value of design from a Classical Design era or the early days of digital design. And so designers who practice design must find new ways to add additional value to their work beyond the practice of design by moving pixels and creating an influx of digital work through platforms, ux, ui, social media, marketing and interactions. Designers have a higher calling to implement greater value to their work, but the current landscape of design doesn't not offer or support these efforts.

And so I call upon designers to reconsider their roles, their titles and their evolution of design. Recognizing that the world exists in a oscillating pendulum swinging back and forth between sincerity and irony, the design now holds a different responsibility. That responsibility to to tie themselves to neither modernism or post-modernist ideals. But to exist between the two. To recognize that their is value and obsurdity in both movements. And from this place we can design between both/and where our work and output and discipline of design creates a new sensibility and value for the world. Where we put the audience first and at the forefront by allowing them to feel a sense of tension, confusing, uncertainty within the familiarity and security of our work. We then create a sense of discovery and meaning for the audience beyond our own desires. Where our work exists beyond a modernist or post-modern sentiment and is rooted in the both/and.

Considering this approach, the landscape of design is rooted in biased ideologies currently. Subscribing to either a modern or post-modern grand narrative within the design community, within our work, and also within the identity of Designers. My thinking here is that we need a new form of Designer I like to call the "Ex-Designer".

The idea of the "Ex-Designer" being an outcast to the old world way of thinking about design, but also encompassing the overall "Experience" of design by any means necessary and exploring those means through the work. "Ex" represents both the deconstruction of the designer and the re-construction of a shift to focus on the experience of design for themselves and for the audience intended. It also represents the intentional effort to detach ourselves from either a "modernist" or "postmodern" sensibility of our work, approach, and identity. So that we can exist within both through a Metamodern lens in which we can build and design the future being self-aware through our work and the intentions in which our work exists.

Ex-Design means that we are thinking deeply about our future. We are considering the next evolution of design beyond a title. Beyond an unregu-lated industry. Beyond cultural bias. Beyond politics. Beyond the current landscape of culture. We are considering the evolution of our discipline to not only being rooted in the work and practice of design, but the inten-tion in which our work and practice takes place. The framework in which we approach our work does not exist within an old-world perspective of either/or, of "modernism" or "post-modernism", but our discipline and practice now emerges from a place where we can observe, evaluate and design holding values and recognizing weaknesses from both "modern" and "post-modern" sensibilities.

In practice, this means that we must have a firm understanding of how "modernism" and "postmodernism" is articulated through our work, creative direction, strategy, deliverables, intentions and put into existence.

I have broken these down into attributes in which we might initially approach design and creative direction to "Look and Feel" and "Messaging and Tone". With these attributes making up a large majority of our work and our direction, by recognizing the tonality and then flipping it on it's head, we can approach our work from a Metamodern lens with new set of creative directions.

Look and Feel Examples:

Modernism
- Bold
- Bright
- Calm
- Chic
- Classic
- Clean
- Confident
- Elegant
- Formal
- Genuine
- Glamorous
- Hand-Crafter
- Historic

- Industrial
- Intellectual
- Inviting
- Masculine
- Minimal
- Modern
- Natural
- Nostalgic
- Organic
- Outdoorsy
- Polished
- Preppy
- Refined
- Relatable
- Relaxed
- Retro
- Rich
- Romantic
- Rustic
- Serene
- Serious
- Sleek
- Soft
- Sophisticated
- Southern
- Strong
- Structured
- Subtle
- Traditional
- Tribal

- Vibrant
- Warm

Post-Modernism

- Adventurous
- Airy
- Artistic
- Breezy
- Bohemian
- Casual
- Coastal
- Comfortable
- Cool
- Cozy
- Cute
- Dreamy
- Earthy
- Ecclectic
- Edgy
- Energetic
- Ethereal
- Feminine
- Fresh
- Friendly
- Fun
- Funky
- Happy
- Irreverant
- Laid back
- Ladylike

- Loud
- Nautical
- Playful
- Quirky
- Sexy
- Unexpected
- Urban
- Whimsical
- Youthful

Looking at both of these lists, we can then build new visual creative directions by combining modern and postmodern attributes to build new directions in our creative work. The list serves as a rough starting point in how we might consider the intentions behind our work through a meta modern lens, where we actively try to capture and imagine the sensibilities of both the modern and the postmodern. As time moves forward, this list will grow, evolve and change over time. The mapping of these attributes will be experimented, explored and created as we move beyond the post-modern world.

For example, we might choose "Bold" and "Industrial" from the Modernism list and "Edgy" and "Irreverent" from the Post-Modernism list. Before beginning any design, we might consider how the attributes of the brand and business related to the audience might create new sensibilities and tensions within the work. Where the experience, aesthetic, messaging, art direction, visual, user experience and interactions encompass oscillating attributes from the above list where we can begin to explore new creative avenues for building a pendulum within our work.

The outcome creates an opportunity for our work to exist between both modern and postmodern attributes where the tension and uncertainty within the work creates an emotional space and new sensibility for the audience to experience the oscillation and allow them to sift through the pendulum and oscillating emotions for themselves. This approach goes beyond the traditional media, marketing, advertising, branding and current digital experiences and expectations - in which the business or brand sets out to determine the response from the audience or selling an idea or belief through positioning, messaging and clever tactics. The inverse of this approach puts the decision making process on the audience in which they get to first experience, feel the tension of metamodernism, and then decide for themselves what they believe to be true or not true about the work. This forces the business and brand to share a deeper respect for their audience and it allows the audience feel as if the business or brand allows them to decide for themselves how they should feel about the world. As audience and consumers have become immune to the old world ways of media and advertising tactics, our propensity for detecting hidden sales agendas, clever marketing tactics and convincing us to buy and consume has become more evolved in the technological era.

From here, our metamodern approach to creating new ideas for a "Look and Feel" might emerge from creating and combining visuals related to:

Bold and Edgy and/or Industrial and Irreverent

Bold - Bright colors, heavy type, all caps, modern and corporate layouts

Edgy - Grunge textures, obnoxious colors, scratches, moving the layouts off-grid

Industrial - Masculine and mechanical typography, palettes of gray and slate colors

Irreverent - Imagery of feminine bodies, young angst, aggression and post-modern ideals

From these directions we can create a balance between the two attributes from Modernism and Post-Modernism and explore those ideas around look and feel. This creates a sense of tension at first, but then the audience gets to sift through those initial reactions and make some sort of meaning for themselves - beyond our own approach in either a modern or post-modern perspective.

We take a different approach to our creative work. We look at design through a lens of creating an emotional platform. We approach the work to present it as a place where the audience can come to experience and explore in a way where the interpretation, feeling and understanding differs from person to person while allowing the heightened sensibility of feeling through a metamodern lens becomes intentionally designed, without bias from designer.

Messaging and Tone Examples:

Modernism

- Authoritative
- Trustworthy
- Sympathetic
- Serious
- Romantic
- Respectful
- Professional
- Passionate
- Nostalgic
- Matter-of-fact
- Informative
- Friendly
- Frank
- Formal

- Casual
- Dry
- Conservative
- Caring

Post-Modernism

- Cheerful
- Coarse
- Conversational
- Edgy
- Enthusiastic
- Fun
- Funny
- Humorous
- Irreverent
- Playful
- Quirky
- Provocative
- Sarcastic
- Smart
- Snarky
- Trendy
- Upbeat
- Unapologetic
- Witty

From these lists, we can begin to create new paths for Messaging and Tone in our work. Related to copywriting, we can then use these to combine with the above visuals to build new sensibility in our design.

For example, we might use "Authoritative" and "Serious" from the

Modernism list

Combined with using "Playful" and "Snarky" from the Post-Modernism list

We can create new ideas and directions for tagline, copy and messaging born our these attributes

Authoritative and Serious - Professional, concise, straightforward, leader

Playful and Snarky - Edgy, aggressive, witty, nonchalant

Let's take a brand example tagline. Home Depot. "More Saving. More Doing"

And let's play with it.

Maybe it becomes something like the following:

"Get it done. Whenever you get around to it."

"For those "Maybe this weekend" projects."

"Consider it done, probably, tomorrow."

By playing with tonality from both modernism and post-modernism, we can start to create new ideas and directions in which culture moves in modern and post-modern movements.

The idea of the "Ex-Designer" exists as being inherently metamodern in the term and the idea. The sincere approach to breaking away from old expectations and idealogies about design while simultaneously being somewhat disruptive and ironic by the term "Ex" as if to say the breaking away is a divorce from the industry in which has fostered and built upon these ideals. I say this as an observation about the term and idea, not to try and force the phase. However, in it's essence, it does represent a metamodern sensibility.

A New Path for the Future of Design

—

If we can observe, recognize, reflect and develop a new sense of self-awareness as a designer, the future role of our work will result in the ability to solve greater challenges, lead through design, and build new meaning in society by understanding the oscillation culture is experiencing through the pendulum of modernism and post-modernism emerging through as metamodernism.

We often compare our internal value in relation to the world with how our external body of work compares and holds up against the validation of other designers. We often apply our meaning and worth to how our work is perceived emotionally in the sense of an art form versus the pragmatic impact and rational in context we seek in the depth of work beyond the surface. We compete the validity of our work the surface context of our work in relation to the validation of inspired work within the world. Don't get caught in the emotional trap of feeling inadequate to other designers

We focus on the milestones and pillars of our work and accomplishments. Yet, the work that goes unnoticed, never makes it to our portfolios or doesn't receive accolades or recognition from others is the very work that hones our craft. It is the work that defines who we are and who we are to become within our pursuit of design. You are the collection of work and experience over time.

Don't get caught in the emotional trap of feeling inadequate to other designers.

We often compare our internal value in relation to the world with how our external body of work compares and holds up against the validation of other designers. We often apply our meaning and worth to how our work is perceived emotionally in the sense of an art form versus the pragmatic impact and rational in context we seek in the depth of work beyond the surface. We compete the validity of our work the surface context of our work in relation to the validation of inspired work within the world.

Our personal body of work is not in competition with other designers. Our work is a contribution to larger pursuit of designing a better world. The perspective of our work should be focused on the humble approach to meeting the needs of those we are designing for and simultaneously aligned with the pursuit of adding value to the labor of design. In congruence with others, we can work within a silo of seeking to design better and grow as an individual while also working to add more value within the design community. Our work oscillates between the individual pursuit of our own body of work and also adding to the value of design within the world as a whole. Our focus to accomplish this must be rooted within true empathy of our desires in our work and simultaneously holding empathy for those we are designing for and the design community as a whole.

We must choose to shift our individual focus of design as one that is not in competition for attention, adoration or admiration for our work, but points to the intentional pursuit of solving greater challenges for others within our work. The best design often goes unnoticed and unseen, whereas good design is often invisible. We must seek to be invisible. We must seek to let our intentional work speak for itself without the desire of trying to out-design others. Our value system changes when we focus our work on others and care less about the admiration of others for our contributions. If we choose to hinge the value of our work on the acceptance, admiration and congratulatory notions of others for our efforts, we become enslaved to the opinions of subjectivity. The alternative is to allow our intentional design efforts lead through impact, solution driven efforts and design thinking that can achieve outcomes to complex challenges within our work. The efforts can only manifest themselves in greater solutions when we shift the value of our work from the subjective acceptance of others, to the objective reality of solution driven design.

As this shift occurs, we begin to forget about comparing our work to others, or fast following trends or seeking the admiration from many. We begin to look at our work from a perspective of empathy, whereas our labor seeks to solve greater challenges.

Context of work is important.

Appreciate other designers and creatives who have solid work. They are helping to contribute to the value of design just as much as your are. We are all on a path to make the world better. Every journey and every path is different. Sometimes, the best work doesn't see the light of day for reason's outside a designer's control. So, if your work isn't as exciting, beautiful, artistic or inspiring as another designer - don't fret or be discouraged. Appreciate the beauty and intention and the overall ethos your work contributes to the value of design. Realize that boring design of layouts and type and UX driven work - if impactful and accomplishing the goals - exceeds what it is meant to do, then those in business will value that work and thinking. That type of design is just as impactful (if not more) than the exciting and inspiring designs you see from other designers.

You are the collection of your work and your experience over time.

We focus on the milestones and pillars of our work and accomplishments. Yet, the work that goes unnoticed, never makes it to our portfolios or doesn't receive accolades or recognition from others is the very work that hones our craft. It is the work that defines who we are and who we are to become within our pursuit of design.

Many times, we celebrate the significant milestones in our career. We highlight the key parts we think others would take notice of. We point to highest marks of competition in our work, whether by way of agency, freelance, collaboration or sheer luck. We point to the collection of companies we've worked with and have worked for. We hope future possible clients who don't yet exist may find us or recognize us or choose to hire us based on our merits.

Of the 20% of my work that I am proud of, the other 80% is still significant, to me personally. I find those moments of work that may never see the light of day, land on my portfolio or never turned out quite the way I wanted, to be just as significant as the work that gets celebrated. For this work, that goes unseen, is the training ground for working with with others, business models, collaborations, creative thinking and problem solving. This work is like those mornings you don't want to go to the gym, but do it anyways. Over time, this work molds my greatest work into what it is.

You are the collection of work and experience over time. Inch by inch.

Our progress and success in design is not celebrated by the pinnacle milestones, but in the journey of our pursuit to create meaningful and purposeful work. We must choose to work away each day at some part of our work and lives to because a better designer. Not purely in the execution sense, but in the process, the approach, the business and the sentiment of what it means to work within design.

The journey is about growth and exploration. But is also about your impact.

Through this pursuit of constant and consistent growth as a designer, we choose to grow and explore many facets of what it means to be a designer. However, this must also be a pursuit of discovering how to have impact. Impact within our work, within our company, within our community and within the world. Our pursuit aligned with a focus of impact will position our trajectory in life as a designer to seek to work on meaningful and purposeful work. Whereas we decide what is important based on our values and align our work and future work to pursue those values within the miopic approach to our work for greater impact on work as a whole.

Design 20 years ago does not look like what design is today. We shouldn't assume that design 20 years from now will look anything like what it is today.

Always evolve. As design changes and new industries have emerged, most of the design practices today did not exist 20 years ago. It becomes important that we simultaneously master our craft and seek to evolve for the uncertain future of design. Our work may not translate into future roles, however, our thinking and approach to design and solving problems will. As we evolve, we learn how to grow and progress from our current state of design into new paradigms of design that do not yet exist. We must be aware of changes within the landscape of technology, design and global economics and prepare our future paths of design to be relevant to new challenges. It is only through the mediums that currently and have yet to exist where we can apply our progressive growth and evolution of design thinking, process and approaches to help create new solutions through the future that has yet to be formed. We are simultaneously creating solutions for the present day to lead us into the uncertain future that will progress from our work in current day.

Find the core foundations of design outside of the tactical execution of the craft

- Design is not software.

- Design is not a collection of fonts.

- Design is not watching tutorial videos.

- Design is not browsing images for ideas and remixing.

- Design is not putting together moodboards and executing based on gut feelings.

These examples are tactics of design, and if they are the core of your design process, then the process is inherently flawed within. The notion and understanding of design in society today is that design is aesthetic and must move quickly to constantly grasp and capture the attention through visual, audio and messaging put forth in an inspiring way. However, this approach within itself becomes a flawed attempt at design, where the aspect of design is about creating better system for humanity, not more noise to keep up with the cultural conversation. If the design and vision is set to be forward focused and innovative, then the time and space to understand the validity of the ideas to move forward must be captured deeper than the execution and tactic of fast moving and focusing on the external narrative of design. This approach is an amateur view and perspective about the use and impact of design. Design is first about people, then systems and process and identifying the challenges in society to create better solutions. Without understanding these key parts, no amount of new aesthetic, new fonts, new tools or fast iteration of creative efforts will create long term sustainability through a flawed perspective of design. It may give short term gains, but it is not sustainable.

Seek to be multidisciplinary.

There is a narrative driven within the creative industry that leadership presents that you should focus on a single sector within the creative field and become a master of this work. However, this is misguided and bad advice.

This is dangerous and misguided.

Do not buy into the narrative that hiring managers and agency leadership are selling you to "focus on a single craft".

Design is solving complex challenges, whereas the singular act of a specific tactic requires the ability to think about solving challenges in complex ways. When our lens is solely focused on a single disciple, we being to look at the challenges and solutions through a single perspective. The alternative is the ability to see the connectivity of multiple disciplines and creative efforts, connect the threads of thinking patterns within those disciplines and apply complex solutions to complex problems through a single tactic. This is the ability to exist at a 30,000 foot view of the landscape and discover how creativity in discovering solutions exists within a single tactic. If we operate within the nuanced perspective of a single discipline, we limit our ability to solve complex problems through our limited perspective. This does not allow design to lead at the forefront of challenges, but to exist as a cog within a wheel of executing as a tactic. However, our perspective of design should not be limited to focusing on a single discipline, but to work diligently at understanding multiple disciplines and applying the thinking across multiple design disciplines in preparation of solving complex design challenges.

This takes away your leverage.

Those in leadership who profess that you must focus on a single discipline and to not be multidisciplinary do not want the best for your career. Instead, they want to maintain power of their own position and hire those who can only serve as singular functions within the larger vision they intend to create. The alternative is working with many multidisciplinary people who are talented at many different things and bring a wide spectrum of ideas and insights to solve challenges through creative thinking, holistic approaches and staying curious within their work.

The message given to young creatives to "not be multidisciplinary" is a power play.

Whereas, we become order takers and not contributors to the greater challenges. Business executives, marketing leaders, and organizational leadership needs the perspective of design to help lead and guide through solving greater and more complex challenges that exist within the world today.

Your work and discipline likely did not exist 30 years ago and their is no promise or guarantee that the discipline you seek to double-down on will be relevant or in demand 30 years from now. You must allow yourself to learn many different ways of designing and creating and solving problems with the intention that how you think about solving problems is more important than how you execute. We live in a digital world where work exists and then is forgotten. We are not focused on making art that will exist for hundreds of years. We are designing solutions to solve problems. These solutions arise from many different avenues and ways of thinking. There is a thread of thought that transcends a single discipline and when understood, you can work through the thinking of any creative discipline and apply your thinking across multiple pursuits. There is no risk in protecting your future and diversifying your creative efforts and design acumen.

I have a strong disregard and reject the message that you should not be multidisciplinary. We must have the ability to see the larger problems and design systems that serve outside of our nuanced perspective. When we choose to focus on a single discipline in design and creative efforts, we are limiting our thinking to look through a single lens and apply that thinking across all other creative and design efforts. The inverse is to be well-equipped and versed in many areas of design and creativity whereas you can connect the patterns of creativity and design throughout multiple disciplines and apply that thinking across nuanced tactics to be carried out appropriately when it serves the needs of the challenges you are solving within your work.

Design is about thinking in systems. To solve challenges both creatively and pragmatically. When you focus on a single discipline, you look through the lens of design from a single nuanced perspective that can be limiting in your capacity to connect the creative dots within your solution driven thinking and also be blind to the notion of creating impactful systems through design because you exist in silo versus thinking both holistically and through the lens of a discipline. When you focus on a single craft within design, you are looking through a siloed lens and then expected to solve systematic problems.

Contradictory to design. When you only focus on the craft of design, you cannot see the integrated parts of business, brand, audience and development. You must build an understanding of all the moving parts to build and innovate in more impactful ways. The moving parts will inform the opportunities and constraints within your work and it will shine a light into the paths of creative problem solving where the real excitement emerges. When you understand the functioning parts of not just your discipline, but the vastness of your own discipline combined with the various segments of the challenge you are trying to overcome, you develop a new lens of thinking creatively to build new solutions that radically innovate and move your work into another hemisphere of opportunity and impact.

Being multidisciplinary makes you future proof.

Learning new tools, understanding how to execute in various mediums and learning to perform various tasks is an excellent skill to have. But more importantly, the ability to learn new tools and skills quickly is even better. With a lens of holistic design and perspective, you can apply your approach, process and thinking across many versions of design practice. The result is that those various practices feed into each other and into your view of design from a systematic, visual, functional, form and development process. This creates a bigger worldview of design where you can see and manage challenges more effectively and better than those who solely focus on a single trade within design. Many times I have heard the term "Jack of all trades, master of none" however, with the amount of information and tools at our expense, we cannot afford to be stagnant. To be a master of one. The Jack's of trades are those who see the connective tissue of design, creativity, functionality, development and systems and can adapt and pivot. The ability to evolve and grow and understand multiple trades does not diminish your value, but makes you more valuable. I have personally saved millions of dollars in mitigating risk for clients, found new opportunities for business growth and generated billions in revenue through platform development specifically because I have explored many disciplines of design and development throughout my career in a way where I am not only creating the end product, but informing the risks and opportunities along the way. This can only occur if you have a holistic perspective about design, brands, business and technology.

Apply foundational design principles, approaches, and thinking to various design disciplines.

You will discover patterns within various design disciplines. These patterns emerge through your process, your intention and your creative thinking as your work through the discipline of design with various disciplines. The patterns exist as nuances and as large holistic truths about design. For example, the details of typography and the foundations of their existence and effectiveness translate to the design and usage of icons. The interactions and desires of humans in physical space translate the interactions and expectations in the digital space - creativity breeds within these truths if you seek to surprise and delight your audience along the way during these experiences. Understanding the connective truths will give you insight and opportunity to create and innovate with intention and delight. Building upon the the connective patterns you can discover by being multidisciplinary is far more effective to the long term sustainability of your design journey versus working to become a master of a discipline that may or may not exist in a decade. The power of your work exists in process, approach, and the translation of information to create new and innovative delightful experiences for others. When you work in a silo, when you live in a silo, when you exist your life in a silo, you short yourself to the possibilities of thinking in new and innovative frameworks that being a multidisciplinary design provides.

Follow the leaders

There has been great foundations, designers, thinkers, and leaders within the design industry over the past 100 years. Learning the foundational principles of design is important, and just as important, learning from the works and thoughts of those designers who have come before you is just as necessary to envisioning a future of design by understanding where it has been.

The following designers are a list of those whom I admire, have studied, learned from and continue to reference their work and thoughts for inspiration.

- Adrian Frutiger
- Alan Aldridge
- Alan Fletcher
- Alexey Brodovitch
- Alvin Lustig
- April Greiman
- Armin Hofmann
- Bradbury Thompson
- Bruce Mau
- Bruno Munari
- Cassandre
- Chip Kidd
- David Carson
- Dick Bruna
- Eddie Opara
- Emil Ruder
- Eric Carle
- Eric Gill
- Erik Nitsche
- Erik Spiekermann
- George Lois

- Giambattista Bodoni
- Hans Hulsbosch
- Harry Beck
- Herb Lubalin
- Herbert Bayer
- Herbert Matter
- István Orosz
- James Victore
- Jan Tschichold
- John Alvin
- John Lloyd
- John Maeda
- Jon Burgerman
- Jonathan Barnbrook
- Josef Müller-Brockmann
- Julian House
- Kate Moross
- Katherine McCoy
- László Moholy-Nagy
- Leif Podhajsky
- Margaret Calvert
- Massimo Vignelli
- Max Ernst
- Max Huber
- Michael Bierut
- Milton Glaser
- Muriel Cooper
- Neville Brody
- Otl Aicher
- Paul Rand

- Paul Renner
- Paula Scher
- Peter Saville
- Philip B. Meggs
- Reza Abedini
- Saul Bass
- Shigeo Fukuda
- Stanley Donwood
- Stefan Sagmeister
- Steven Heller
- Storm Thorgerson
- Susan Kare
- Tibor Kalman
- Vincent Connare
- Wally Olins
- William Morris
- Wim Crouwel
- Wolfgang Weingart

What is the alternative of comparing our work to others?

If we compare our work and it's value to others, we will never actualize and manifest the opportunity of working towards creating the work that has yet to exist within us. If our work in design is a lifelong journey to make the world a better place, our work should be a reflection of that pursuit and the continuous journey to fulfill that work at every juncture. If we compare our work to others for the measurement of it's validity, we are not being true to our self and we are not allowing our own work to have value and grow.

Our intention as designers and creators should be built on the idea that we are striving to be the best version of ourself. Our work is a never ending process of growth, evolution and new perspectives of how to look at the world and humanity. Over the course of your career you will seek to design things that garner attention, but as time roles on, the shift happens where you seek to design for impact. Creating work that has immense purpose does not have to attract the attention of the design community or the recognition of others. Our journey is our own and design is a tool and practice that creates opportunities for us to contribute to building meaningful things for humanity. Our job is not to compare our work with others, but to compare our work with the impact we seek to have through our work.

Intention vs execution

Intention must be examined. The reason behind what drives the work. The meaning of why the work is existing or will exist is just as important to understand, examine and define as much as the work itself.

There are those in the metamodern way of thinking who believe that metamodernism is defined by the execution. The examination of the external parts of a piece are not the determining factors of deciding if a work is metamodern. Many so called "scholars" of metamodernism are getting this wrong.

Metamodernism is about the intention and the oscillation of the execution. Meaning that the intention must be first understood and the execution should strive for aesthetic oscillation of the intention.

The intention can be sincere or ironic. If choosing the be sincere, the execution should find ways to be ironic against the sincerity of the intention. If the intention is to be ironic, the execution must find ways to create sincerity within the irony.

Within the execution you can then find new ways to oscillate between grand narratives against itself to drive a work forward. This is where I believe so many people fail to recognize and examine Metamodernism at its true form. The most powerful forms of metamodernism are the works which oscillate sincerity and irony between the intention and execution.

Suspended between sincerity and irony.

Metamodernism relies on the oscillating balance of a body of work to suspend itself between sincerity and irony. Many have tried to identify this by comparing the external parts of a body of work against each other to make comparisons and find the contrasts. However, I believe this is a false observation and we should be weary to accept these proclamations about metamodernism.

Metamodernism is about the simultaneous oscillation of sincerity and irony happening within a work. Yes. But the way the work was manifested, created and put into the world takes on a part of either the sincerity or the irony of the work in of itself. Therefore, we must look at the intention behind the work. The way the work was created. How the work was thought through and the execution through that work aligned with either it's own sincerity or irony in it's incubation. This is where I believe most have failed to identify true metamodernism.

As a creator, metamodernism takes on an entirely different meaning versus the audience. The metamodernism is not strictly within how the audience feels, but also how the work makes the audience feel within the confines of how the work was created. If the work was sincerely made but forces the audience to receive it as ironic while understanding the sincerity of the execution - that is metamodern. However, I have seen where metamodernism is defined on the external constructs of the work making the audience feel one way or another while dismissing the creation of the work itself playing a major role in defying the work itself as metamodern.

How a work was created is a part of metamodernism that has yet to be defined. For example, a sincere message for a brand on a social media post combined with some post-modern imagery is not metamodern. It's post-modern. However, that same message executed in a different way by the brand may become metamodern. For example, the message could be handwritten, or typed on a typewriter and scanned, or audio from a sincere letter or message to invoke the same emotion. Point being: the way the message aligns to the visual communication in of itself becomes a defining piece of how metamodern something is.

Personal impact of metamodernism

Through observing culture through a design lens and coming to discover the sensibilities align with the idea of metamodernism, I have learned and developed a few key personal ideas and evolution of myself during this process. I'd say that my journey has existed through observation and seeking to recognize and define these movements in culture since around 2007 after I stepped into the real world as a designer. But even before then, my observations go back to the early days of my teenage years where I was playing in punk rock bands, skateboarding and growing up in a small town outside of Seattle.

Metamodernism has become a tool to unpack and define observations about the world. It has become a tool to observe and identify truth's within the world, and also truth within myself. I have evolved more as a person by recognizing the oscillation within this new global society. The polarity of ideals, morals, virtue signaling, economics, politics and religions have built a new perspective in which I view the world from.

Recognizing the oscillations in culture allows me to explore ideas, philosophies and narratives within modern and post-modern ideologies. Existing within both cultural movements, I find myself going back and forth between mainstream media, news, articles and joining panels and discussions and communities with vastly different viewpoints from the far left to the far right. I engage with a wide variety of people who exist in both places where I find the opportunities to listen and learn from their perspectives.

The exploration of defining this sense of unrest as "Metamodernism" led to discerning my own views of the world where "both-and" can exist. Where if we choose one side of the pendulum or the other in this growing global cultural narrative, we are forced to rationalize and follow a "side". However, I think the skeptic with myself has led me to look at the larger challenges both places of modernism and post-modernism exists and seek to understand the pro's and con's of each. From this, I have very differing views politically, religiously, economically where the focus of my own thinking exists in the continuity of logical thinking - applying the same logic across every touch point where the polarity of modernism and post-modernism of today find themselves in contradictory and hypocritical rationale.

I have developed a new found discovery of the importance of faith, spirituality and the belief in God. Apart from the expected ideals we understand in the modern religious systems. Or the abandonment of any religion whatsoever. I believe there is a deeper meaning and truth beyond the validity or historical accuracy of the Bible in which exists a grand narrative if we choose to unpack it for ourselves. I find it absolutely captivating in many ways. And if you look at the broader message of the Bible, the designed story framework and the underlying intention applied metaphorically to our own lives in modern day - it becomes a truly beautiful book in which to apply living. I've gone the other path for many years, believing that my life and success is completely up to me. And that is true. But the greater purpose beyond a narrative rooted in modernism or post-modernism provides a better framework in which we can navigate our own lives.

I have seen the value of social justice, socially liberal ideas - however I don't agree with the narrative and execution around them. I work and have worked with many companies, organizations, and businesses in the social justice space. From art collectives, Fortune 100 companies, Financial institutions, health and wellness companies and non-profits. I 100% value the efforts of their greater purpose, however, I believe there is a greater purpose and meaning beyond the tonality in which we create. That both/and can exist in these conversations. A win-win. A place where there doesn't need to be a villain to have a hero. A place in which equality of opportunity reigns supreme and the ability for the individual to discover their own purpose beyond a narrative.

I have seen the importance of embracing traditional values around family, home, and traditional means of belief and thinking. Whereas, the idea of progressive policy and ideology has not lost it's value, but it has a time and place within our society. It becomes dangerous for us to consider the homogenization of culture through a battling between modernism and post-modernism. I find value in both and see the benefits of modernist ideals related to traditional values, beyond the rhetoric of political agendas. The practicality of these ideals hold a form of truth in which can withstand the narrative between modernism and post-modernism and exist as a place to build a foundation for a solid life.

I see the value of disruption through a postmodern lens, but I believe it can be applied in different ways to build a better world. As a Designer, it is within our nature to observe the world through a skeptical lens. But as I grow older, I realize that this skepticism does not equal cynicism. I believe it to be healthy to positively look at ways in which disruption can be a tool, not the means to an end. Disruption in capitalism creates opportunities for free markets. Disruption in technology creates new paths of job creation and innovation. Disruption in work life balance creates new ways of living and increasing our quality of life for a more sustainable humanity. Disruption of economics means that we can reassess and improve upon ways in which we trade and value goods and services.

Disruption is not bad in which it is meant to build and create and expand new opportunities and paths for advancement of humanity as a whole. Disruption becomes a problem when the focus has no other means but to disrupt without the follow up of discovering new solutions to challenges.

Metamodernism has created a space where I can exist as the individual where ideologies from opposing sides of culture can exist. Choosing to agree or disagree with a set of cultural thoughts or ideas does not make me a patriarchal-mysognist-alt-right-toxic-masculine male, nor does the belief in certain liberties for those whom are not like me make me a bleeding heart idealistic progressive concerned with furthering the agenda of the deep state. There exists a balance between the extreme polarities in which we are currently experiencing in culture at a local and global level.

Both/and can exist within cultural narratives. For me, "both-and" represents the deep universal sentiment of love and truth that dates back thousands of years and is embedded in cultural, historical and religious stories we have been experiencing and hearing for years.

There is an ancient truth and modern ideals for the future of design to build upon.

We must have the courage to step within ourselves first before we can decide to impact the world through design.

Reference List

1. Abramson, Seth. (January 9, 2017) "What Is Metamodernism?" [Website] Retrieved from https://www.huffpost.com/entry/what-is-metamodernism_b_586e7075e4b0a5e600a788cd

2. Associated Press (2020) Divided America [Website] Retrieved from https://www.ap.org/explore/divided-america/

3. Australian Government (2014) The market for design: insights from interviews with Australian firms [Website] Retrieved from https://www.ipaustralia.gov.au/sites/default/files/ip-australia-economic-research-paper-03.pdf?acsf_files_redirect

4. Bogdan, C. (2012, August 14) New French Extremity: An Exigency for Reality. [Website] Retrieved from http://www.metamodernism.com/2012/08/14/new-french-extremity-an-exigency-for-reality/

5. Cameron, J. (2016, October 25) The Artist's Way: 25th Anniversary Edition

6. Clarke, J (2015, April 16) "The Role of the Graphic Designer in a Metamodern Structure of Feeling". [Website] Retrieved from https://www.metamodernism.com/2015/04/16/the-role-of-the-graphic-designer/

7. Craig, James, Bevington, William, Korol Scala, Irene (2006, May 1) Designing with Type, 5th Edition: The Essential Guide to Typography

8. Cooper, Brent (April 10, 2018) On Metamodern Leaderhip [Website] Retrieved from https://medium.com/the-abs-tract-organization/on-metamodern-leadership-87bcf9ada5f9

9. Cooper, Brent (April 10, 2018) The Metamodern Condition [Website] Retrieved from https://medium.com/the-abs-tract-organization/the-metamodern-condition-1e1d04a13c4

10. Davis, D. (2016, June 14) Creative Strategy and The Business of Design

11. Dalio, R. (2017, September 19) Principles: Life and Work

12. Dalio, R. (2019, November 26) Principles for Success

13. Design Census (2019) Designcensus.org [website] Retrieved from http://designcensus.org

14. Design Council (2009) Design Industry Research 2010 [Article] Retrieved from https://www.designcouncil.org.uk/sites/default/files/asset/document/DesignIndustryResearch2010_FactSheets_Design_Council.pdf

15. Deeley, D. (September 26, 2019) Five Examples of Postmodernism in Television [Website] Retrieved from https://www.theodysseyonline.com/examples-postmodernism-television

16. Donald, N (1988) The Design of Everyday Things

17. Duignan, B. (September 4, 2020) Postmodernism. [Website] Retrieved from

18. Dun & Bradstreet (2020) Graphic Design Service Industry Insights from D&B Hoovers [Website] Retrieved from https://www.dnb.com/business-directory/industry-analysis.graphic-design-services.html

19. Elam, K. (2007, April 19) Typographic Systems of Design

20. Elam, K. (2005, August 1) Grid Systems: Principles of Organizing Type

21. Enns, B. (2010, July 6) Win Without Pitching

22. Freinacht, H. (2015, February 16) 5 Things That Make You Metamodern. [Website] Retrieved from https://metamoderna.org/5-things-that-make-you-metamodern/

23. Freinacht, H. (N.D.) What is Metamodernism? [Website] Retrieved from https://metamoderna.org/metamodernism

24. Archiv, Bauhaus, Droste, Magdalena (2006, June 1) Bauhaus 1919-1933

25. Gordon Worley III, G (2017, Aug 18) Embracing Metamodernism. [Website] Retrieved from https://mapandterritory.org/embracing-metamodernism-5d4ebe8a8ddf

26. Ghosh, Iran (September 25, 2019) Charts: America's Political Divide 1994-2017 [Website] Retrieved from https://www.visualcapitalist.com/charts-americas-political-divide-1994-2017/

27. Gladwell, M. (2011, June 7) Outliers: The Story of Success

28. Gladwell, M. (2002, January 7) The Tipping Point: How Little Things Can Make a Big Difference

29. Graham, B. (2006, February 21) The Intelligent Investor: The Definitive Book on Value Investing. A Book of Practical Counsel (Revised Edition)

30. Griffith, Robert [WIkipedia] Retrieved from https://en.m.wikipedia.org/wiki/Roger_Griffin

31. Harari, Y.N. (2018, May 15) Sapiens: A Brief History of Humankind

32. Hsieh, T. (2013, March 19) Delivering Happiness: A Path to Profits, Passion, and Purpose.

33. IBISWorld (2020) Graphic Designers Industry in the US - Market Research Report [Website] Retrieved from https://www.ibisworld.com/united-states/market-research-reports/graphic-designers-industry/

34. IIT Institute of Design (2020) 100 Great Designs of Modern Times [Website] Retrieved from https://id.iit.edu/projects/100-great-designs-of-modern-times-2020/

35. IMDB (2020) Postmodern [Website] Retrieved from https://www.imdb.com/search/keyword/?keywords=postmodern

36. Interbrand (2018) Best Global Brands 2018, Activating Brave

37. Jencks, C. (1977). The Language of Post-Modern Architecture. New York: Rizzoli.

38. Kilkilley, M. (April 15, 2016) 5 Ways Computational Design Will Change the Way You Work [Website] Retrieved from https://www.archdaily.com/785602/5-ways-computational-design-will-change-the-way-you-work

39. Krogerus, M., & Tschäppeler, R. (2018, May) The Decision Book: Fifity Models for Strategic Thinking (Fully Revised Edition)

40. Kuiper, Kathleen. Modernism. Retrieved from https://www.britannica.com/art/Modernism-art

41. Lupton, E. (2004, April 16) Thinking with Type: A Primer for Designers: A Critical Guide for Designers, Writers, Editors, & Students

42. M. Hardt and K. Weeks. (2000). The Jameson Reader. Oxford: Blackwell Publishing, pp, 190-191.

43. Maeda, J (2020) CX Report

44. Maeda, J (2015) Design in Tech Report [PDF file]. Retrieved from https://designintech.report/wp-content/uploads/2018/11/designintech2015.pdf

45. Maeda, J (2016) Design in Tech Report [PDF file]. Retrieved from https://designintech.report/2016/03/13/design-in-tech-report-2016/

46. Maeda, J (2018) Design in Tech Report [PDF file]. Retried from https://designintech.report/wp-content/uploads/2019/01/dit2018as_pdf.pdf

47. Maeda, J (2019) Design in Tech Report [PDF file]. Retrieved from https://designintech.report/2019/03/09/design-in-tech-report-2019/

48. MacDowell, J. (2011, July 19) Quirky, Tone and Metamodernism. [Website] Retrieved from http://www.metamodernism.com/2011/07/19/quirky-tone-and-metamodernism/

49. McKinsey (2018) McKinsey Design Index [Website] Retrieved from https://www.mckinsey.com/business-functions/mckinsey-design/our-insights/the-business-value-of-design

50. "Modernism" (September 2020) In Wikipedia. Retrieved from https://en.wikipedia.org/wiki/Modernism

51. "Metamodernism" (September 2020) In Wikipedia. Retrieved from https://en.wikipedia.org/wiki/Metamodernism

52. Wikipedia (2020) "Metamodernism" [Website] Retrieved from https://en.wikipedia.org/wiki/Metamodernism

53. Neumeier, M. (2003) The Brand Gap: How To Bridge the Gap Between Business Strategy and Design

55. Olsen, & Scott (2006, October 16) The Golden Section: Nature's Greatest Secret

56. Osterwalder, A. (2014, October 20) Value Proposition Design: How to Create Products and Services Customers Want (Strategyzer)

57. Peterson, J. (2018, January 23) 12 Rules for Life: An Antidote to Chaos

58. Pendergast, Augusta (N.D.) Understanding Modernism and Post-Modernism [Website] Retrieved from http://pendau01.sites.gettysburg.edu/how_do_we_fit_in/understanding-modernism-and-post-modernism/

59.Pew Research Center (2020) Political Polarization [Website] Retrieved from https://www.pewresearch.org/topics/political-polarization/

60. "Postmodernism" (September 2020) In Wikipedia. Retrieved from https://en.wikipedia.org/wiki/Postmodernism

61. Quintana, Xela (October 13, 2018) Culture: Metamodern Pairs with Millenials [Website] Retrieved from https://www.logosmagazinecc.com/culture-metamodernism-pairs-with-millennials/

62. RGD (2017) Packaging Design Industry Insights [Website] Retrieved from https://www.rgd.ca/2017/12/20/packaging-insights.php

63. Rogan, Joe (Producer). (2016, November 28) Joe Rogan Experience #877 - Jordan Peterson [Audio podcast]. Retrieved from https://www.youtube.com/watch?v=04wyGK6k6HE

64. Rogan, Joe (Producer). (2018, July 2) Joe Rogan Experience #1139 - Jordan Peterson [Audio podcast]. Retrieved from https://www.youtube.com/watch?v=9Xc7DN-noAc

65. Rogan, Joe (Producer). (2018, July 2) Joe Rogan Experience #993 -

Ben Shapiro [Audio podcast]. Retrieved from

66. https://www.youtube.com/watch?v=UQTfyjhvfH8&list=LLWtsErBo
TRpfqtjfuttDyGg&index=755

67. Rogan, Joe (Producer). (2017, October 10) Joe Rogan Experience
#1022 - Eric Weinstein [Audio podcast]. Retrieved from https://www.
youtube.com/watch?v=lMzjEaNFbAk

69. Rickards, J. (2016, January 1) The Big Drop Second Edition How To
Grow Your Wealth During the Coming Collapse

70. Rustad, G. (2012, February 29) Metamodernism, Quirky and Femi-
nism*,   http://www.metamodernism.com/2012/02/29/metamodernism-
quirky-and-feminism/

71. Samara, T. (2005, May 1) Making and Breaking the Grid: A Graphic
Design Layout Workshop

72. Sazon, Gladys Jean (August 18, 2016) Modernism-Post Modernism
Timeline [Presentation] Retrieved from https://prezi.com/qso4uvkwf3mf/
modernism-post-modernism-timeline/

73. Schroeder, A. (2009, October 27) The Snowball: Warren Buffet and the
Business of Life

74. Seib, G. The Wallstreet Journal (December 17, 2019) How the U.S.
Became a Nation Divided [Website] Retrieved from https://www.wsj.com/
articles/how-the-u-s-became-a-nation-divided-11576630802

75. Sheperd, S. (November 26, 2018) The inescapable postmodernism within Television series Community [Website] Retrieved from https://medium.com/@sam.shepherd/the-inescapable-postmodernism-within-television-series-community-df5c9f527f07

76. Sosolimited (March 2, 2017) 5 Insights About The Current State of Design [Website] Retrieved from https://medium.com/sosolimited/5-insights-about-the-current-state-of-design-d1ae85880960

77. Spiekermann, E. (2013, December 23) Stop Stealing Sheep & Find Out How Type Works, Third Edition

78. Toth, J. (2010). The Passing of Postmodernism. New York: State University of NewYork, p. 2

79. Turner, L. (2011) "The Metamodernist Manifesto" http://www.metamodernism.org/

80. Turner, L. (2012, July 2) The New Aesthetic's Speculative Promise. [Website] Retrieved from http://www.metamodernism.com/2012/07/02/the-new-aesthetics-speculative-promise/

81. Turner, L. (2012, September 12) David Foster Wallace's Hideous Men & London's Olympic Epiphany. [Website] Retrieved from http://www.metamodernism.com/2012/09/12/david-foster-wallaces-hideous-men-londons-olympic-epiphany/

82. Vermeulen, T., & Van den Akker, R. (2010) "Notes on Metamodernism"

83. Sullivan, E. (2014, November 24) Miranda July: Interrupting the Conventions of the Personal. [Website] Retrieved from http://www.metamodernism.com/2014/11/24/miranda-july-interrupting-the-conventions-of-the-personal/

84. Whalley, C. (2014, August 5) I Love Roses When They're Past Their Best. [Website] Retrieved from http://www.metamodernism.com/2014/08/05/i-love-roses-when-theyre-past-their-best/

85. Williams, R. (1977). Marxism and Literature. Oxford: Oxford University Press, p. 131

86. USHistory.org (2019) 4a. American Political Culture [Website] Retrieved from https://www.ushistory.org/gov/4a.asp

87. University of Salford, Manchester (2009) Design 2020 [Website] Retrieved from http://usir.salford.ac.uk/id/eprint/12618/1/Design2020_final.pdf

END

ABOUT THE AUTHOR

Jordan Wayne Lee is an Emmy® Award Winning Designer, Certified Brand Strategist, Creative Director, Front-End Developer and Musician.

He has worked for brands such as Disney, ESPN, Apple, Netflix, Universal Studios, Hulu, REI Co-Op, SEOMoz, TEDx, Amazon Video, UBS, Annie Leibovitz, CAA, and many others. In addition, he has worked with a number of non-profits, startups, record labels, creative agencies, celebrities, public figures and private businesses in retail, finance, venture capital, music and entertainment.

He earned his Bachelors degree from Lee University in Cleveland, TN. with a minor in Biblical Theology and later studied Design Thinking at Cornell University, Ithaca, NY. He studied Brand Strategy under Marty Neumeier, Level C, of San Jose CA.

He grew up in Marysville WA, a small rural town outside of Seattle, and currently resides in Los Angeles with his wife Laura.

He is the founder of Neon Wilderness, a brand strategy and design firm located in Los Angeles, CA.

www.jordanwlee.com / www.metamodern.ist